Introduction to Post-Keynesian Economics

Also by Marc Lavoie

MACROÉCONOMIE: Théories et controverses post-Keynésiennes

FOUNDATIONS OF POST-KEYNESIAN ECONOMIC ANALYSIS

MILTON FRIEDMAN ET SON ŒUVRE (co-edited with Mario Seccareccia)

AVANTAGE NUMÉRIQUE: l'argent et la Ligue nationale de hockey

DÉSAVANTAGE NUMÉRIQUE: les francophones dans la LNH

CENTRAL BANKING IN THE MODERN WORLD: Alternative Perspectives
(co-edited with Mario Seccareccia)

Introduction to Post-Keynesian Economics

Marc Lavoie

First published 2006 by
PALGRAVE MACMILLAN
Houndmills, Basingstoke, Hampshire RG21 6XS and
175 Fifth Avenue, New York, N.Y. 10010
Companies and representatives throughout the world

PALGRAVE MACMILLAN is the global academic imprint of the Palgrave
Macmillan division of St. Martin's Press, LLC and of Palgrave Macmillan Ltd.
Macmillan® is a registered trademark in the United States, United Kingdom
and other countries. Palgrave is a registered trademark in the European
Union and other countries.

ISBN 13: 978–0–230–00780–2   hardback
ISBN 10: 0–230–00780–5   hardback

This book is printed on paper suitable for recycling and made from fully
managed and sustained forest sources.

A catalogue record for this book is available from the British Library.

A catalogue record for this book is available from the Library of Congress.

10   9   8   7   6   5   4   3   2   1
15   14   13   12   11   10   09   08   07   06

Printed and bound in Great Britain by
Antony Rowe Ltd, Chippenham and Eastbourne

Contents

List of Figures

List of Tables

List of Boxes

Preface to the English Edition

This book is a slightly modified version of the work that first appeared in French as *L'Économie postkeynésienne* (Paris: La Découverte (Repères), 2004). Besides a few updates and additional references here and there, changes are mainly to be found at the end of the last three chapters, where I have extended the discussions of work sharing programmes, inflation control, and policies against unemployment.

I am very grateful to my fellow post-Keynesian colleague Basil Moore for having forcefully encouraged me to submit a translation proposal to Palgrave Macmillan. Mrs Delphine Ribouchon, from La Découverte, was also highly helpful in arranging for the translation rights. I am thankful to my research assistant, Jung Hoon Kim, who compiled the index. Finally I would like to thank my Canadian colleague Louis-Philippe Rochon, who translated the manuscript, graciously forgoing his own research for a while, as well as his Christmas vacations.

Introduction

The idea of writing a synthesis of post-Keynesian theory first came to me during one of my brief visits to France. While in Paris, I visited bookstores in the Latin Quarter, near the Sorbonne, and, to my surprise, discovered that they all contained a number of economics books that condemned what the French call 'la pensée unique' (the single thought), or what the English-speaking world knows as 'There Is No Alternative' (TINA). The various authors were all indignant at the economic policies adopted by governments, central banks and the large international institutions, such as the IMF and the World Bank.

According to their advocates, the austerity measures put in place, which include deregulation and privatization, aim to limit the problems of inflation, preserve the exchange rate, increase the rate of growth of productivity and create permanent jobs. While the objectives are certainly not controversial, the ways in which they are pursued raise suspicion. Stemming from a free-market ideology which includes the so-called Washington Consensus, these economic means have become today's conventional wisdom – which is just as controversial as the conventional wisdom that John Kenneth Galbraith (1958) was ridiculing more than four decades ago. Free-market advocates propose a long list of policies, including an independent central bank that is free to set high interest rates (as was the case with the European Central Bank), weak unions, greater labour market flexibility, wage restrictions, and reductions in both public services and tax rates. They also propose balanced budget amendments, or the quasi-elimination of fiscal deficits, as in the Treaty of Maastricht and the Stability Pact, which gave birth to the New Europe and that still constrain the public expenditures of member countries. Finally, one could add to this exhaustive list the privatization of large public companies and the dismantling of many market regulations. The objective is quite simple: to make markets as flexible as possible, which, the proponents argue, will benefit society in the end.

The failings of the Washington Consensus have been well documented by its opponents. Yet, I have often found the various critiques of the Consensus unconvincing. While virtually all of the dissenting research is quite good in showing the shortcomings of neoclassical theory, it falls short of proposing any serious alternative. Even some neoclassical economists, such as Joseph Stiglitz (2002, 2003), categorically reject many of the free-market policies that were adopted during the 1980s and 1990s, readily admitting that such policies rest on an oversimplified neoclassical theory and that better developed neoclassical models convincingly demonstrate the limitations of such policies.

A new alternative theory

I do not believe that offering a tortuous critique of the dominant view is the best strategy. Many critics of free-market economic policies start with the neoclassical economic model and its tenuous theoretical foundations, onto which they superimpose some assumptions taken from the real world. Yet, this approach only yields models that are increasingly difficult to grasp.

This book uses a very different approach. My objective is quite clear: to present a true alternative to the dominant school of economic thought which contradicts and rejects the main tenets of free-market advocates. This alternative is post-Keynesian theory.

Mainstream textbooks, those that are imposed on first-year economics students nearly everywhere, do not usually discuss post-Keynesian economics. Students often stumble upon it in courses in the history of economic thought, or in classes dealing with theories of growth and fluctuations, in large part due to the Cambridge models of growth and distribution suggested by Joan Robinson, Nicholas Kaldor and Luigi Pasinetti. Economists or students of political economy may also come across post-Keynesian theory when discussing the famous 'capital controversies', which date back to the 1960s. It is usually within this context that post-Keynesian economics is associated with Sraffian or neo-Ricardian economics. Moreover, post-Keynesian theory is often portrayed as negative, restricted to demonstrating the limitations and deficiencies of the neoclassical production function or of other theoretical constructs such as total factor productivity growth.

Yet, since the 1970s, great strides have been made. There is now a large body of research, covering many different fields, based on post-

Keynesian economics. This body of work shows that post-Keynesian economics, besides having disproved key neoclassical theoretical constructs, has developed key ideas of its own, on the theoretical, empirical and policy fronts. Several post-Keynesian surveys or books have been published that underline this positive contribution. Some academic journals, such as the *Cambridge Journal of Economics* (created in 1977), the *Journal of Post Keynesian Economics* (1978) and the *Review of Political Economy* (1989), have exclusive or substantial post-Keynesian content, while many others, such as the *Review of Radical and Political Economics*, often include post-Keynesian articles.

There are also organizations, such as the *Post Keynesian Study Group* in the United Kingdom or the *Association des Études Keynésiennes* in France, that are devoted to post-Keynesian studies and that organize or sponsor regular workshops or conferences. And there are also economics departments that run graduate programmes devoted to post-Keynesian economics and other heterodox views, such as the New School University, the University of Missouri in Kansas City, the University of Massachusetts, Amherst, or the University of Utah. Finally, there has been a regular Post-Keynesian summer school, which allows students from all over the world to meet post-Keynesian scholars.

An antidote to TINA

Post-Keynesian economics is an effective antidote to TINA – the belief that mainstream economics and its free-market solutions are the only way to understand and solve economic problems. It offers a strong theoretical foundation which can serve as a basis for criticism of mainstream theory and its austerity policies, as well as supporting the proposition of feasible alternative policies.

While post-Keynesian theory, like neoclassical theory, has microeconomic foundations, its theoretical foundation is different and, in many ways, more realist. Moreover, the macroeconomic policies stemming from these microeconomic foundations are radically different to those founded in neoclassical theory.

In the following chapters, we will concentrate on debunking a number of myths that arise from an elementary application of neoclassical theory (see Keen, 2001). Consider the following counter claims, which will be demonstrated in this book: a rise in demand does not necessarily increase prices; a rise in the minimum wage or in the real wage does not lead to an increase in unemployment; an increase in the real wage does not lead to a fall in profits; a decline in the saving rate leads neither to a fall in investment nor to a slow-down in the growth rate of the economy; a flexible price system does not bring the economy back to the equilibrium (or optimum) level of output; and finally, budget deficits lead neither to inflation nor to a rise in the rate of interest.

Many label economics the 'dismal science' because of the assumption made by mainstream theorists that society must suffer under austere policies, and that unrestrained competition must be championed in order to achieve economic nirvana. In contrast, post-Keynesian theory offers a radically different message – in my view a more positive and more exciting message: cooperation, rather than competition or conflict, will lead to better results. Scarcity is in fact a mere intellectual construct that can be cast aside (Ventelou, 2001).

In favour of a post-autistic economics

In the year 2000, a number of students from various universities in France took a stand against the way in which economics was being taught, thereby leading to a movement that has since spread to other countries as well (Fullbrook, 2003). This movement has inspired the creation of a network and a newsletter – the *Post-Autistic Economics Review* (found at http://www.paecon.net/) – that has over 8000 subscribers in more than 150 countries.

Students criticized the dogmatism of their teaching and the irrelevance of formalized models that seemed to relate to some imaginary world rather than to the real world. Hence, they referred to these teachings as 'autistic'. They demanded courses that would better teach them the limitations and shortcomings of neoclassical theory. They also requested more pluralism, and the inclusion of some heterodox teachings that would reflect the real world.

This book is dedicated to these students and their followers. Its objective is to contribute to their struggle.

1
Post-Keynesian Heterodoxy

1.1 Who are the post-Keynesians?

Post-Keynesian economics is only one of many heterodox schools of thought. Within this heterodox label, of which most members are clearly opposed to neoclassical economics, we find Marxists, Sraffians (also called the neo-Ricardians), neo-Structuralists (on development issues), Institutionalists, the French Regulation School, Humanistic or Social economists, Behaviourists, Schumpeterians (also called Evolutionists), Feminist economists, and more.

Heterodox economics is subjected to two opposite forces. First, heterodox schools suffer the general implosion of science, and of economics in particular. Each heterodox approach has tended to emphasize particular questions in an effort to distinguish itself from other approaches. While heterodox schools are all rivals, they are nonetheless complementary, by targeting a particular aspect of the economy.

Second, there is also a counter-tendency toward unity among heterodox schools, perhaps as a result of their status of minorities in peril. Indeed, many heterodox scholars look for interactions and unity between the approaches. This is particularly true of American post-Keynesians and neo-radicals (Marxists), who work in macro-economics and monetary theory. In fact, one particular organization, the International Confederation of Associations for Pluralism in Economics (ICAPE) plays host to all heterodoxies as well as their institutions and journals. As such, the contours of the different approaches are to some degree arbitrary.

As their name indicates, post-Keynesians find their principal inspiration in the work of John Maynard Keynes, the famous British economist at the University of Cambridge. In fact, many claim that his 1936 book, *The General Theory of Employment, Interest and Money*, gave birth to macroeconomic theory.

And yet the book led to a number of conflicting interpretations. Post-Keynesians, for instance, have an interpretation that is different from that of economists like Paul Samuelson and James Tobin, and the rest of the so-called 'neoclassical synthesis' Keynesians. It also is quite different from the interpretation given by the 'new Keynesians', such as Gregory Mankiw, Alan Blinder and Joseph Stiglitz (see Figure 1.1).

Modern post-Keynesians, however, do not limit themselves to Keynes. They are also inspired by the work of those who were close to Keynes at the time he wrote the *General Theory* at Cambridge – such as Roy Harrod and Joan Robinson – and by those who were instrumental in creating the Cambridge School in the 1950s and 1960s. Among these economists, we have Nicholas Kaldor, Michal Kalecki and Piero Sraffa. The views of post-Keynesians, like those of several authors of the French Regulation School (Boyer, 1990), are closely tied to the work of Institutionalists, especially those inspired by the ideas developed by Thorstein Veblen and John Kenneth Galbraith. In this sense, they continue the work started in 1936 by the Oxford Economists' Research Group. But, like Keynes, post-Keynesian economists are generally concerned with macroeconomic issues.

1.2 The characteristics of heterodox economics

Before we begin describing the main features of post-Keynesian economics, it is important to discuss what makes heterodox economics different from neoclassical economics. Listing the defining features of neoclassical theory is not, however, an easy task. Indeed, what is the glue that unites those who study neo-Walrasian general equilibrium models with those who use game theory or even those who are neoclassical synthesis Keynesians?

Neoclassical economists themselves often refer to the principle of constrained maximization as a unifying theme, and it is no doubt a central component of the approach. Until recently, we could even

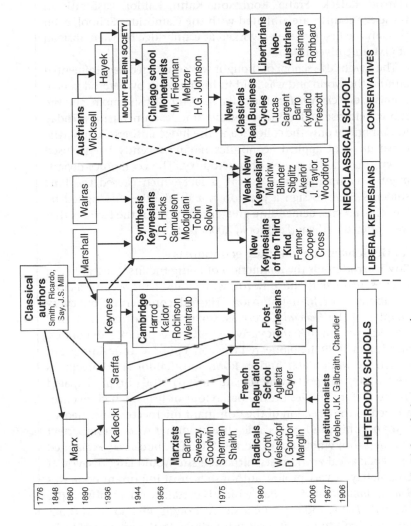

Figure 1.1: Schools of thought in macroeconomics

Box 1.1: Post-Keynesians in England

The Cambridge School
Harrod, Kalecki, Sraffa, Robinson, Kahn, Kaldor, Pasinetti: all these economists are affiliated with the Cambridge School, even though the first two never worked at Cambridge but were instead at Oxford University.

The Cambridge school of thought was considered very influential around the world and was held in high esteem by heterodox economists, especially before the collapse of the British Empire and the subsequent rise to dominance of the American universities. Today in Cambridge only the colleges and the Judge Business School (the department of applied economics having recently been closed down) maintain a degree of heterodoxy. The economics department is completely neoclassical, a fact which caused the PhD students there to sign a petition not unlike the one signed by French students, demanding greater pluralism in the lectures that were offered to them (Fullbrook, 2003, p. 36).

A brief look at the founding economists
Roy Harrod holds the distinction of being the first biographer of Keynes. Just like **Richard Kahn**, who would later become a close collaborator of Joan Robinson, Harrod commented on every chapter of the *General Theory* as Keynes was writing it. Harrod was known for his innovative work in economic dynamics. Starting in 1939, he pioneered the concept of technical progress, which we would later find in Robinson, Kaldor and Kalecki, as well as in many post-Keynesian authors. Harrod also participated in the Oxford studies on the behaviour of firms, which eventually led to the rejection of the dominant microeconomic theory.

Joan Robinson first became known for her work on imperfect competition, which appeared in 1933. The book was acclaimed by neoclassical economists, although she would later disavow it completely. A very prolific author, her most important book was *The Accumulation of Capital*, which is certainly on a par with the *General Theory*, and a great classic. Although the book is at times quite difficult to read, it deals primarily with the choices of techniques of production, monetary questions, issues of distribution, and the problems concerning a constant rate of growth without unemployment.

Box 1.1: Post-Keynesians in England – *cont'd*

Robinson, along with Sraffa, was one of the principal architects behind the 'Cambridge controversies', which questioned the neoclassical concept of capital and the dominant theory of distribution (Cohen and Harcourt, 2003).

Nicholas Kaldor, was also at the heart of the Cambridge revolution. Of Hungarian descent, Kaldor arrived in England in 1927. His ideas were constantly evolving, and he contributed to innovations in a number of important fields. For instance, he offered innovative theories on speculation, multiple equilibria and virtuous circles. He also contributed significantly to theories of growth and development, as well as to questions concerning monetary policies and public finance. While he never attempted to synthesize his own work, many authors today still find inspiration in his theoretical and empirical work.

Michal Kalecki, a Polish economist, lived in England between 1936 and 1946, where he developed a close friendship with Joan Robinson. Many economists claim that he is the father of the principle of effective demand. Moreover, and contrary to Keynes, Kalecki's macroeconomic theories did not rest on Marshallian microeconomic foundations. Kalecki was foremost an econometrician, and his work focused on business cycles. In fact, many early econometric Keynesian studies were inspired by his work.

Piero Sraffa was born in Italy but arrived in England in 1927. Sraffa was known for his early critique of Marshallian economics, especially the theory of supply in a purely competitive environment. Not a great teacher, he soon embarked on editing the complete works of David Ricardo. In doing so, he began trying to resolve some of the problems raised by Ricardo (which is the reason why Sraffian economics is often referred to as neo-Ricardian economics), in particular the famous problem of the measurement of value, linked to the determination of relative prices in a world where the production of commodities is the result of a circular process. His work would culminate with the publication of *The Production of Commodities by Means of Commodities* (1960), which Sraffa sees as a prelude to a criticism of neoclassical theory. Many Italian economists converged on Cambridge under Sraffa's supervision, the most influential ones

---

Box 1.1: Post-Keynesians in England – *cont'd*

being **Pierangelo Garegnani** (1990) and **Luigi Pasinetti** (1981, 1993), whose work dealt, respectively, with the theory of capital and uneven sectoral growth. Such was the influence of these three authors that for a while the post-Keynesian school was known as the Anglo-Italian school. Pasinetti (2005) now speaks of 'the Cambridge School of Keynesian Economics'.

Information on other post-Keynesian authors can be found in the biographies edited by Arestis and Sawyer (2002). In his book on the history of post-Keynesian economics, King (2002) carefully traces the history of post-Keynesian authors up to today, and offers, in King (1995b), an exhaustive bibliography.

In addition to the book edited by Holt and Pressman (2001) and the various post-Keynesian dictionaries (see for instance King, 2003; and Arestis and Sawyer, 1994), there exist a number of general textbooks on post-Keynesian economics. Consider the following, in order of difficulty: Reynolds (1987), Arestis (1992), Lavoie (1992a), Eichner (1987) and Palley (1996). Finally, there is a complete survey of post-Keynesian monetary economics (Arestis and Sawyer, 2006).

---

claim that the principle of diminishing returns, so enshrined in microeconomic teachings, was a central element of neoclassical economics. Yet, the new neoclassical models of endogenous growth assume away decreasing returns.

If we wish to compare the neoclassical school with the heterodox schools, we need a more global approach. In fact, we must step back a little. About 30 years ago, a well-known economist, Axel Leijonhufvud (1976), suggested studying what he called 'presuppositions'. These are the essential elements of a given school of thought, which cannot be formalized or modelled, and in fact pre-date the various hypotheses and theories that derive from them. Some methodologists claim that presuppositions are the sum of the metaphysical beliefs that constitute a paradigm (a research programme). In the next section, we will try to identify these so-called presuppositions.

We can differentiate the neoclassical approach from heterodox approaches – including post-Keynesian theory – by referring to four methodological categories, to which we will add a political element (see Table 1.1). Among the presuppositions of neoclassical theory, we find an instrumentalist epistemology, methodological individualism, unbounded (substantive) rationality, and an exchange economy based on the scarcity of goods.

Heterodox economics, however, emphasizes realism, organicism (holism), procedural rationality and a production economy. These differences are far from being arbitrary. In fact, we find them in almost identical forms in the descriptions of various methodologists and heterodox authors (Lavoie, 1992b; Setterfield, 2003). The political presupposition will be discussed later.

Realism vs instrumentalism

Instrumentalism is the dominant epistemology (the science of learning) of neoclassical economics. For instrumentalists, a hypothesis is sound for two reasons: it is acceptable, first, provided it allows for accurate predictions, and, second, as long as it can help to calculate the value of a new equilibrium position. The realism of any particular hypothesis is not of concern. Theories are mere tools or instruments of analysis, largely regardless of their ability to explain the real workings of the economy.

This is precisely the epistemology defended by Milton Friedman, among others, and endorsed by the vast majority of neoclassical authors.

Table 1.1: Presuppositions of the neoclassical and heterodox research programmes

	Paradigms	
Presuppositions	Heterodox approaches	Neoclassical approach
Epistemology	Realism	Instrumentalism
Ontology	Organicism	Individualism
Rationality	Procedural rationality	Substantive rationality
Focus of analysis	Production, growth	Exchange, scarcity
Political core	State intervention	Free markets

On the other hand, most heterodox authors consider the realism of the hypotheses as extremely relevant to economics. The objective of economics is to be able to tell a relevant story and to explain the way the economy actually works in the real world. To do this, we have no choice but to begin with reality and its various stylized facts, rather than starting from a hypothetical idealistic position. And while all theories are to some degree abstractions of the real world, which means that they are in a way imperfect and simple, they must nonetheless be descriptive; they must depict the real world, and not some imaginary one.

In fact, there is no doubt that the most common criticism of neo-classical theory is that it is not a realist or realistic depiction of the real world. To be fair, there are hints of realism embedded within neoclassical theory. But these tend to be auxiliary hypotheses removed from the theoretical foundation of neoclassical theory that depicts a non-existent ideal world. Heterodox economists, on the other hand, consider this approach as misleading and far removed from the real world: it rests on an imaginary view of the world.

Organicism and methodological individualism

At the heart of neoclassical theory is the individual – the economic agent. While this was obvious in the Walrasian general equilibrium theory, it is even more obvious under the guise of the new macro-economic reconstruction of neoclassical theory, which requires microeconomic foundations resting on the representative agent, who is simultaneously consumer and producer, and who maximizes whatever function under some constraints. Moreover, institutions such as banks or firms only hide the true intentions and preferences of individuals. This is a world of atomized agents – the world of methodological individualism.

The heterodox approach, on the other hand, is worlds apart. Individuals are viewed as social beings, under the influence of their environment, including their culture and social class, as underlined by Marxist authors. Moreover, the microeconomic decisions of individuals can give way to macroeconomic paradoxes, such as the well-known paradox of thrift.

As for institutions, they have a life of their own. They are not the mere reflection of the various desires of the individuals within them. They also have their own objectives. The old adage is true: the whole is more than the sum of its parts.

Organicism, or holism, at least a moderate version of it, is the cornerstone of the heterodox approach. In fact, the new mathematics associated with chaotic dynamics, based on non-linearity and strange attractors, breathed new life into this conception of science, since the analysis of chaotic dynamics requires a global approach.

Note as well that institutions are not perceived as imperfections or impediments to the market system. On the contrary, institutions bring stability to the economic system as a whole. Power relationships and asymmetries come to the fore. These then encourage the study of income distribution among the various social classes, or among the various institutions that hold power within society, such as banks and large corporations. They also encourage us to look more closely at the relationships between economic sectors and the constraints that they impose upon each other.

Procedural and substantive rationality

In neoclassical theory, economic agents possess an absolute or substantive rationality. In many ways, we could argue that this is a rather unreasonable presupposition, since agents apparently possess quasi-unlimited knowledge and ability to calculate economic outcomes. The introduction of a lack of perfect information in certain neoclassical models only serves to reinforce this unreasonable ability of agents to calculate and optimize information. This hyper-rationality is akin to the concept of rational expectations that we find in 'new classical' or new Keynesian models.

For heterodox economists, however, rationality is bounded or procedural, in the sense used by Herbert Simon (1976). Individuals and institutions face severe limitations in their ability to acquire and process information. This inability goes beyond the existence of imperfect information, as we find it in neoclassical economics where agents are also able to factor in the time spent searching for the optimal quantity of information. For heterodox economists, however, the information is often insufficient or indeed non-existent, which forces individuals and firms to postpone crucial decisions. In fact, these decisions are particularly difficult to make, given that they depend on expectations of the future, which itself depends on the decisions and actions taken today.

Given this state of affairs, individuals and firms often settle on a 'satisficing' outcome, since no one knows, or can know, the optimal solution. In such a world, or rather to deal with these situations, individuals give themselves norms to follow; they rely on conventions, customs, rules of behaviour and rules of thumb, or imitate actions taken by neighbours or individuals who are in the limelight, whose behaviour they imagine to be better informed; or else they create institutions to reduce the detrimental consequences of uncertainty. Rules of thumb are not ad hoc; rather they are a rational response to an uncertain and often complex environment.

Production and scarcity

Following Lionel Robbins, the most common definition of economics is the efficient allocation of scarce resources. This definition, however, only applies to neoclassical theory, where indeed the scarcity of goods dictates economic behaviour; anything that has value must be scarce and hence confronted to an opportunity cost. Prices only reflect scarcity.

The concept of exchange dominates neoclassical theory. The auxiliary hypotheses that we find in more sophisticated models of production simply reinforce once again the conditions and implications of a pure exchange economy. Producers follow the laws of arbitrage and operate within an otherwise glorified exchange economy.

By contrast, for heterodox economists, production supersedes exchange. As is the case in the works of classical authors such as Adam Smith or Karl Marx, heterodox economists are primarily interested in the need to create the necessary resources that will contribute to greater production and wealth. At the heart of this analysis is the existence of a surplus, and the causes of growth in employment, production and technical progress, which will then contribute to an increase in the quality of life. To be fair, these issues are also discussed at times by neoclassical economists and their models of endogenous growth. But in heterodox economics, since full employment of resources is not assumed, the discussion of their efficient allocation is not a major issue.

Rather, what is emphasized among post-Keynesian economists is the degree to which these resources are utilized. In this sense, the economy usually operates within the boundaries of the production possibility frontier, which is itself quite flexible. As a result, there are always opportunities for a free lunch. Furthermore, even if one assumes that full employment is reached, heterodox authors argue that a number of innovations will most likely push back this natural frontier. Economists therefore should not focus on the allocation of scarce resources; rather they should concentrate on going beyond scarcity, when, and if ever, scarcity arises.

The political presupposition: the view on markets

The above list of presuppositions would not be complete if we did not include a discussion over the relative attitudes of neoclassical and heterodox economists towards markets. While heterodox authors recognize that ideology drives economic research and even data-gathering activities, neoclassical authors pretend that their theories are free of any ideology.

The majority of neoclassical economists favour free enterprise and laissez-faire, having faith in the ability of market mechanisms – the so-called invisible hand – to drive the economy to optimal results. While this is a general statement, it must be recognized of course that some neoclassical economists do build models that show that capitalist economies based on a price system can lead to instability and sub-optimal results. But these models are viewed as anomalies. In fact, all neoclassical economists believe that if it were possible to rid markets of the various imperfections that limit competition and the availability of perfect information, flexible prices would bring back the economy to a perfect equilibrium.

Neoclassical economists often present their argument in the following way: in the short run, because of the presence of some imperfections or externalities, state intervention may be needed. In the long run, however, markets are perfectly flexible, being able to guarantee equilibrium on their own, and hence a minimal level of state intervention is optimal since the state is a source of inefficiencies in the long run.

While neoclassical economists place their faith in market mechanisms and the invisible hand, heterodox economists question the wisdom of relying blindly on markets. To various degrees, they question both the efficiency and fairness of market mechanisms, as well as their assumed existence. The inequity of markets is particularly emphasized by social and humanist economists. Moreover, it is impossible to have 'free' markets since they cannot regulate themselves. This was made evident in 2002 with the massive financial frauds of corporations such as Enron and Worldcom. This leads heterodox economists to argue overwhelmingly that markets – especially financial markets – must be regulated by the state, just as private property – which is the foundation of capitalism – must be protected by the state.

As a result, heterodox economists see pure competition, which is beneficial to all, as simply a transitory situation. Soon enough, competition will lead to oligopolies and monopolies. Governments must intervene or position themselves within the sphere of private markets, otherwise instability will set in, which would lead to the squandering of resources. The state must regulate markets, and at the macroeconomic level, it must regulate aggregate demand.

1.3   The essential characteristics of post-Keynesian economics

All heterodox approaches share the presuppositions presented above. If this is the case, what then distinguishes post-Keynesian economics in particular from other heterodox schools?

If we rely on the surveys written by some of its most prolific writers (Eichner and Kregel, 1975; Arestis, 1996; Palley, 1996; Pasinetti, 2005), seven characteristics of post-Keynesian economics can be brought to light.

The first two characteristics – effective demand and historical time, which are to be found in virtually all accounts of post-Keynesian economics – are probably the most essential. The remaining five elements are more auxiliary in nature, and are the result of either the first two essential characteristics or of the presuppositions discussed above. Consequently, not all post-Keynesians consider them as equal in importance; and other schools also adopt some of these elements.

The principle of effective demand

According to the principle of effective demand, the production of goods adjusts itself to the demand for goods. This principle is at the heart of all post-Keynesian approaches. The economy is therefore demand-determined, and not constrained by supply or given endowments. This means that investment is essentially independent of saving; investment and capital accumulation are not tied to the intertemporal consumption decisions of households (Shapiro, 1977).

Of course, many other economists also share this view, although only with regard to the short period. Marxists and new Keynesian economists in particular readily admit that in the short run output and national income are governed by changes in aggregate demand. In the long run, however, both Marxists and neoclassical economists claim that the economy is strictly under the constraints imposed by supply conditions.

In the neoclassical aggregate demand/aggregate supply model, this is depicted by a vertical aggregate supply curve in the long run. This implies, of course, that the economy cannot, in the long run, produce at higher levels of output, regardless of prices. In the context of the Phillips curve, this same reasoning is depicted by a vertical Phillips curve at a given natural rate of unemployment or at the prevailing NAIRU (non-accelerating inflation rate of unemployment). This natural rate is unique and independent of any actual level of unemployment, past or present.

Moreover, if we consider the Solow growth model, long-run growth is limited only by the growth rate of the active population and the rate of technical progress, assumed to be exogenous. In a similar fashion, the long-run rate of growth in Marxist models of accumulation is limited by the rate of saving on profits as well as the normal profit rate, both being supply-side determined variables.

What sets post-Keynesians apart is their refusal to accept the notion that the long run is in any way constrained by supply. Hence, for post-Keynesians, the principle of effective demand is always relevant, both in the short and in the long run. Investment always causes saving, rather than the reverse. In this sense, there are a number of possible long-run positions, which depend on the constraints imposed by effective demand and the existing institutions. It is the supply side that will finally adjust to the demand side.

Dynamic historical time

Inspired by Joan Robinson (1980), post-Keynesians often emphasize the difference between historical and logical time. In the case of the latter, economists hardly ever ask how the economy transits from one equilibrium position to another. Some parameter of the system is modified, demand or supply curves are moved around. It is assumed that the move from one position to another occurs almost instantaneously. Once at the new intersection – the so-called equilibrium – economists proceed to compare the properties of the new position with the old one, and draw from that analysis all sorts of conclusions. When the parameter is modified back to its previous value, the economy returns to where it was, as if time was not a factor. Logical time has no depth.

Historical time is quite different. Time is irreversible: once a decision is made and implemented, it cannot be reversed, except perhaps at a great cost. This is particularly the case with fixed costs, such as investment in a new plant. If there is a true scarce resource, it is surely time.

From this, we can only conclude that any given long-run position is not independent of the short run: it is simply the result of a series of short-period positions (Kalecki, 1971, p. 165). Hence according to post-Keynesians, the path taken by an economy during the transition, following any given shock, is extremely important. As Halevi and Kriesler (1991, p. 86) claim, long-period analysis in logical time is only relevant when 'some coherent dynamic adjustment process is specified which can describe the "traverse" from one equilibrium position to another, without the traverse itself influencing the final equilibrium position, that is, without the equilibrium being path determined'. In general, therefore, post-Keynesians believe that the long period does not exist independently of the path taken during the transition from one equilibrium position to another.

This leads quite naturally into the need, advocated by post-Keynesians, for developing dynamic models of the economy which emphasize the evolution through time of the stocks of physical assets and financial wealth. These models also need to explain the changes in the productive structure of the economy. This is the very essence of dynamic time.

To be sure, the notion that the equilibrium position is not independent of the path of the economy is not a new idea. In fact, Keynes, and a number of post-Keynesians, such as Kaldor and Hyman Minsky, advocated these views a long time ago. Interestingly enough, whereas these ideas were once thought to be difficult to formalize, today they are at the heart of more recent developments in non-linear mathematics, based on the notions of hysteresis, path-dependency, irreversibility and lock-in effects (such as the adoption of QWERTY or AZERTY keyboards). Of course, this all amounts to the possibility of multiple equilibrium positions. And while post-Keynesians are not the only economists to hold these views, these ideas are intrinsically tied to their vision of the economic process.

In addition to the heterodox presuppositions discussed above, consider the key features of post-Keynesian theory outlined in Table 1.2.

Table 1.2: Main features of post-Keynesian economics, beyond the presuppositions of heterodox economics

Essential features	
Effective demand	The economy is demand-determined both in the short run and the long run; supply adapts to demand. At all times, it is investment that determines saving, rather than the converse.
Historical and dynamic time	We must always consider the transition from one position to another, and recognize that the conditions under which this transition occurs may affect the final position of equilibrium.
Auxiliary features	
The possible negative impact of flexible prices	Because of income effects, price flexibility may worsen the situation that it was meant to correct.
The monetary production economy	Models must recognize that contracts are denominated in money; that firms have debts and households have assets that may impose considerable financial constraints.
Fundamental uncertainty	The future is necessarily different from the past. The future is unknown and unknowable since decisions taken today will alter the way the future looks.
Relevant and contemporary microeconomics	Post-Keynesian microeconomics rests on decisions of a lexicographic nature and on inversed L-shaped cost curves (see Chapter 2).
Pluralism of theories and methods	Reality can take several forms. As such, there are a number of different methods as well as economic theories that may appear to rival one another.

The auxiliary post-Keynesian features

In addition to the two essential characteristics just discussed, post-Keynesians often refer to additional specific features when describing their approach. There are five such features and they are the possible destabilizing effects of price flexibility; the existence of a monetary production economy; fundamental uncertainty; relevant microeconomics; and a pluralistic approach to theorizing. The microeconomic foundations will be discussed in the next chapter.

Post-Keynesians reject the tenet of the virtues of flexible prices that is at the heart of neoclassical theory. They tend to downplay the importance of substitution effects – where consumer and producer choices are tied to changes in relative prices – favouring instead the consideration of income effects, where these same choices are primarily determined by changes in income and technical progress.

In fact, post-Keynesians argue that flexible prices can be destabilizing. For instance, while neoclassical economists believe that a decrease in nominal and real wages will bring the economy back to full employment, post-Keynesians think that such actions will only make matters worse. This is because a reduction in either nominal or real wages will impact negatively on effective demand by reducing the purchasing power of workers, thereby increasing the debt burden of firms.

These debts are unavoidable in a monetary production economy. Contemporary economies rest on the existence of contracts denominated in money, in dollars or pounds sterling, for instance. They are not measured in terms of output. Households do not directly own the physical assets of large corporations. Rather they own financial assets, and their desire to part with the less liquid of these can trigger a financial crisis.

At the heart of the post-Keynesian economy is investment, decisions on which are taken by entrepreneurs and firms, independently of the level of saving in the economy. In this sense, the role of banks is of great importance, since they advance to firms the funds needed to begin the production process. Post-Keynesians argue that banks advance the necessary funds to firms as long as they are deemed creditworthy – an assessment which in turn depends on the debt load of firms. This is Kalecki's principle of increasing risk, which is of crucial importance in capitalist economies. Funds advanced to firms – as well as the rate of interest charged on loans – will depend largely on whether the economy is or is not expanding. This is related to the liquidity preference of banks.

Fundamental uncertainty

Liquidity preference is often tied in with fundamental uncertainty, which is usually associated with the writings of Keynes and Frank Knight. Fundamental uncertainty is very different from probabilistic risk, which we find in the neoclassical literature. Under a situation of fundamental uncertainty, it is impossible to calculate either the probabilities of an event occurring or possible outcomes. The future is unknown and unpredictable. What matters then is the agents' confidence – their 'animal spirits', as defined by Keynes.

The notion of fundamental uncertainty is linked to two other important concepts in post-Keynesian theory: historical time and bounded rationality, implying only limited knowledge of the world. In historical time, the future is – or can be – different from the past or the present. In language borrowed from physics, the world is non-ergodic, meaning that the averages and the fluctuations observed in the past will not necessarily be observed in different time periods (Davidson, 1988). Every crucial decision, as defined by G.L.S. Shackle, destroys ergodic processes which may have existed at the moment these decisions were taken.

Non-ergodicity therefore casts doubt on any conclusions or predictions we may make based on statistical analyses or econometric studies. It is less than likely that events we observe today will reproduce themselves in the future.

The most fundamentalist post-Keynesians, such as Davidson and Minsky, believe that the existence of fundamental uncertainty completely destroys the foundations of neoclassical theory. While fundamental uncertainty is certainly pervasive in the real world, neoclassical authors assume away its existence, and they continue to use probability density functions. In fact, Nobel laureate Robert Lucas (1981, p. 224) claimed that 'in cases of uncertainty, economic reasoning would be of no value', meaning here the reasoning of neoclassical theory. It is in this context that Davidson (1984, p. 574) writes that the guiding motto of post-Keynesian economists is: 'it is better to be roughly right than precisely wrong'. It is better to describe the real world with some rough accuracy than to describe an imaginary world with great precision.

Some authors believe that introducing fundamental uncertainty leads to nihilism. This argument rests on the notion that if indeed fundamental uncertainty is pervasive, with the future unknown and unknowable, then it is ultimately impossible to know whether any given economic policy would have its desired effects.

But such an argument can easily be countered. Except in periods of crisis, uncertainty tends instead to create a degree of continuity. Agents and institutions are disinclined to alter their behaviour substantially when faced with news and surprises of all sorts (Heiner, 1983). People will hesitate to act on account of the lack of proper information.

1.4 The various strands of post-Keynesian theory

Pluralism of methods and ideas

Reality can take several forms, which in itself explains why heterodox economists adopt a variety of methods and theories. This is the inevitable result of adopting a realist epistemology, which according to Dow (2001), is particularly the case with post-Keynesians. Yet, this can be both an advantage and a disadvantage, since it often gives the impression that post-Keynesian theory lacks coherence. This was, for instance, the criticism made by Walters and Young (1999).

The last characteristic of post-Keynesian theory is pluralism – that is, pluralism of ideas and methods. Post-Keynesians welcome the contributions of other approaches and schools. For instance, post-Keynesians are open to the ideas of humanist economists on consumer theory, or those of the institutionalist economists on the theory of the firm.

Like economists belonging to the French Regulation school or to the French Conventions school, post-Keynesians derive inspiration from a variety of sources: from economists such as Marx, Keynes, Kalecki, Kaldor, Leontief, Sraffa, Veblen, Galbraith, Andrews, Georgescu-Roegen, Hicks or Tobin, or from other disciplines (sociology, history, political science, psychology and anthropology). The unifying theme is that truth can take several forms. All methods, formal or literary, are acceptable.

Box 1.2: A Post-Keynesian Nobel laureate?

Many economists believe that Joan Robinson and Nicholas Kaldor should have been awarded the Bank of Sweden Nobel Prize for economics before their deaths in 1983 and 1986 respectively. But a post-Keynesian economist, William Vickrey, an American born in Canada, was awarded the Nobel Prize in 1996 for his work on the role of information. He died only three days after the announcement.

The members of the Academy would surely have been surprised to hear his acceptance speech. In the last 12 years or so of his life, Vickrey had been participating in all of the conferences and seminars organized by a well-known post-Keynesian – Paul Davidson, the founder (with Sidney Weintraub, his former teacher) of the *Journal of Post Keynesian Economics*. In fact, Vickrey (1997) believed that the biggest problem in contemporary economies was a structural lack of aggregate demand. As a result, full employment required substantial fiscal deficits. Vickrey was vehemently opposed to restrictions placed on fiscal deficits, such as is the case with the Treaty of Maastricht.

Fundamentalists, Sraffians and Kaleckians

Post-Keynesian theory is far from being a homogeneous approach. In fact, three separate strands can be found: the fundamentalists, the Kaleckians and the Sraffians (Hamouda and Harcourt, 1988).

Fundamentalists, such as Davidson (1972) and Minsky (1976), draw their main inspiration from Keynes. They emphasize fundamental uncertainty, money, liquidity preference, financial instability and methodological questions. These authors, who are sometimes referred to as American post-Keynesians, argue that post-Keynesian theory is more general than neoclassical theory. In order to prove this point, they are ready to entertain certain dubious neoclassical assertions, such as the 'law' of decreasing returns.

Sraffians, of course, are inspired by the work of Pierro Sraffa, as well as Marx, although indirectly. They are mainly concerned with relative prices, the choices of techniques and the interdependence inherent in the existence of a multisectoral production system, as in input–output analysis. Sraffian theory is also labelled as the 'surplus approach' since their models also assess the surplus from inter-mediate production.

Sraffian work has also emphasized joint production (for instance meat and lambswool), the measure of fixed capital and the choice of an invariable anchor of value. These highly technical questions nevertheless generated a substantial amount of interest among heterodox economists and even the lay public (at least in Europe) in the 1970s, and this for two reasons. First, Sraffian theory invalidates the neoclassical theory of distribution (Garegnani, 1990; Pasinetti, 1977). Second, it casts doubt on a simplified Marxist theory of labour value (Steedman, 1977). Sraffian theory, as it can be found in Pasinetti (1981, 1993), may nonetheless be viewed as a last-ditch attempt to preserve some version of the labour theory of value, albeit a more coherent and sophisticated one.

Finally, the third strand in post-Keynesian economics is the Kaleckian approach (Sawyer, 1989). While they are inspired pri-marily by Kalecki, Kaleckians are also indirectly influenced by Marx (especially that part in Marx that deals with the problem of the realization of profits), and more directly by Kaldor and the Insti-tutionalists. Kaleckians are very eclectic (King, 2002, p. 219). They are as interested in microeconomics, for instance the pricing pro-cess, as they are in macroeconomic aggregates and mesoeconomic financial relations.

In contrast to fundamentalist post-Keynesians, however, Kaleckians do not see their approach as more general than neoclassical theory, but simply as more realistic and relevant to a greater number of circumstances and industries.

While many post-Keynesian authors will claim allegiance to a given approach, some will certainly admit to being influenced by all three post-Keynesian strands. Among the more eclectic post-Keynesians, we find Alfred Eichner (1987) and Edward Nell (1998).

The greatest differences between post-Keynesians arise when we compare the views of Sraffians with those of fundamentalists (Arena, 1992), in particular when contrasting the reasons under-pinning their criticisms of neoclassical theory. For fundamentalists, neoclassical theory is wrong because it does not incorporate fund-amental uncertainty, the lack of ergodicity, and the features asso-ciated with a monetized economy of production. For Sraffians, however, neoclassical theory ought to be rejected because the 'real' side of the theory is incorrect, since neoclassical theory rests on an adjustment mechanism that relies on flexible factor prices (real wages, real interest rates), which is presumed to reflect relative scarcities – a claim that Sraffians have proved to be mistaken.

The Sraffian critique, as Robinson (1980) observed, is often lost on fundamentalists and Kaleckians since it represents an internal critique of neoclassical theory, and does not incorporate some essential post-Keynesian features, such as historical time.

Should we exclude some approaches or emphasize others?

Some fundamentalist post-Keynesians believe that it is a strategic mistake to attempt to integrate all three strands of post-Keynesianism (Davidson, 2005). Also, recent attempts at summarizing post-Keynesian theory (see for instance Holt and Pressman, 2001) tend to exclude the contributions of Sraffians because their methods and the themes they cover are considered distant from those of other post-Keynesians. Although I do not specifically address here most of the core themes of the Sraffian school, I nonetheless prefer to include them in my own definition of post-Keynesianism, and this for two reasons. First, there are strong historical and personal ties between a number of post-Keynesians and Sraffians. Second, and perhaps more importantly, whenever Sraffians discuss macroeconomic issues, they adopt models that are similar to those proposed by post-Keynesians.

When we go beyond the realm of criticism and discuss the positive contributions of each approach, we realize in fact that there exists a strong consensus among all approaches, particularly with respect to the importance of the principle of effective demand (King, 1995a, pp. 244–5). For instance, the employment model used by the Sraffian Gary Mongiovi (1991), based on effective demand, gives us results that are similar to those obtained from Kaleckian models (see Chapter 4). Moreover, Sraffian economist Heinz Kurz (1994) uses a growth model with effective demand that is a variation of the Kaleckian model of growth (see Chapter 5). Dutt and Amadeo (1990) in their analysis of the links between all three approaches refer in fact to 'neo-Ricardian Keynesians'.

There are also other points of convergence. When discussing the shape of cost curves (compare for instance the work of Sraffian economists Roncaglia (1995) and Schefold (1997, ch. 17) with the

Box 1.3: Post-Keynesians or new Keynesians?

In the last few decades, there has emerged within neoclassical theory a 'new Keynesian' approach that has adopted, in many respects, a rather critical tone towards 'new classical' economics and unrestricted free-market advocates. What then are the links between new Keynesians and post-Keynesians? This is certainly not an easy question to answer (see Rotheim, 1996). At first glance, we may conclude that new Keynesians are neoclassical authors since they use the same tools of analysis as their new classical adversaries. Yet, like the post-Keynesians, new Keynesians do not constitute a unified approach.

We can identify three main strands within the new Keynesian school. The first two strands are sometimes called *weak* new Keynesianism, as in Figure 1.1. The first strand tries to explain the stickiness of certain nominal variables, which are believed to be imperfections that amplify economic fluctuations. In this sense, the economic policy proposals of the new Keynesians of the first kind are very similar to those of their new classical cousins.

The second new Keynesian strand, within which Stiglitz would be found, attempts to explain the stickiness of real variables, usually by advocating the presence of asymmetric and imperfect information. For the new Keynesians of the second kind, in the short run the flexibility of wages and prices is unhelpful in recovering the optimal properties of the economic system.

Finally, one can encounter new Keynesianism of the third kind, also called post-Walrasian economics by Colander (2003). In this strand, authors build models with multiple equilibria, which are usually attributed to problems of coordination. While this latter approach is influenced by general equilibrium theory and often relies on rational expectations, it is nonetheless closest to post-Keynesian theory since it ends up questioning the existence of a natural rate of unemployment or of a unique natural rate of growth (Van Ees and Garretsen, 1993). Indeed, since these models generate complex and chaotic dynamics, one could argue, as does Rosser (1998, p. 293), that they are self-destructive because they demonstrate the 'unlikeliness of rational expectations actually obtaining in the real world', and that they provide clear foundations for fundamental uncertainty.

Box 1.3: Post-Keynesians or new Keynesians? – *cont'd*

A certain amount of convergence also exists with respect to empirical work, in particular when it comes to dealing with monetary policy and investment functions. In fact, these two fields now incorporate liquidity constraints, largely influenced by Kalecki. One of the leading advocates of this approach, Steven Fazzari, who is known as a new Keynesian empirical author by his mainstream colleagues, is in reality a Kaleckian economist!

Nonetheless, it is clear that new Keynesians and post-Keynesians differ significantly when we consider the role played by constrained optimization and by effective demand in their respective models (Dutt, 2003). For post-Keynesians, effective demand is both dominant and crucial, whereas for new Keynesians aggregate demand is usually exogenous; constraints mainly appear from the supply side.

---

content of Chapter 2) or the workings of monetary economies, we can see that there are close affinities between Sraffians and post-Keynesians. Indeed, some Sraffians, such as Carlo Panico (1988), adopt an endogenous money framework and believe that the central bank can only control the short-term rate of interest – two themes that are central to fundamentalists and Kaleckians (see Chapter 3). Moreover, Sraffians like Roncaglia (2003) offer an analysis of the prices of natural resources, in particular the price of oil, which does not rest on any notion of scarcity. In fact, it rests on radical uncertainty and a given rate of technical progress, again concepts that are key in post-Keynesian theory.

A warning is in order. The following chapters tend to favour the Kaleckian rather than the fundamentalist strand of post-Keynesian economics. There are several reasons for this. First, the Kaleckian approach offers a clear, realistic and coherent view of effective demand. Second, the degree of formalization required to understand this approach is ideal for the readers of this book. As such, the Kaleckian approach represents the perfect antidote to TINA. Third, the Kaleckian model is extremely flexible. It has proved common ground for many heterodox economists (Marxists, Sraffians, structuralists and regulationists) who have modified it to build their own version. Fourth, the Kaleckian model is well-suited for empirical and econometric research, having been derived, as already pointed out, from an author – Kalecki – who was himself an econometrician.

Finally, just like Kaleckians, I will try to be eclectic and discuss themes that are of interest to all post-Keynesians.

2
Heterodox Microeconomics

Neoclassical microeconomic theory is closely tied to two important concepts in economics: marginalism and decreasing marginal utility, suggesting that the more we acquire of a given good, the less additional utility we derive from it. Accordingly, if the importance we assign to any good is directly related to its total utility, the price of that good is related to the additional utility we receive from it – marginal utility. This is marginalism.

The first neoclassical economists modelled production theory on consumer theory. The principle of diminishing returns is the carbon copy of the principle of decreasing marginal utility. Yet, while students are often in awe of the similarities between the laws governing consumers and firms, these are not the result of any natural process; rather they are an artificial construct that arises from the fancy for symmetry of the first neoclassical authors.

Post-Keynesian theory rejects indifference curves as well as neoclassical convex isoquants with their famous U-shaped cost curves. Moreover, the rules and behaviour that govern entrepreneurs and consumers are quite different from those we find in neoclassical theory.

2.1 Consumer choice theory

To develop their theory of consumer choice, post-Keynesians turn to a number of sources, including the work of psychologists, socio-economists, institutionalists, marketing specialists and the work of such economists as Nicholas Georgescu-Roegen (1966) or Herbert

Simon and the behaviorist school. In fact, Drakopoulos (1992) has shown that Keynes himself could be associated with this alternative consumer theory, which does not rest on an axiomatic approach, relying instead on observed behaviour. Indeed, Fontana and Gerrard (2004) argue that the results of recent experimental studies by economists and psychologists on decision-making under uncertainty are clearly supportive of the post-Keynesian approach.

Before discussing the post-Keynesian theory of consumer choice, however, it is important to distinguish clearly between wants and needs. Modern neoclassical economists are often confused when it comes to distinguishing between the two concepts, which was ironically not the case of their predecessors, such as Alfred Marshall and Carl Menger. Quite simply, needs can always be ranked and prioritized – there is a hierarchic ranking of needs – whereas wants evolve from needs and constitute 'the various preferences within a *common* category or level of need' (Lutz and Lux, 1979, p. 21). This distinction can be best represented with the following analogy: while thirst is a need, the choice between Coke and Pepsi is purely the result of the desire for one cola over the other.

Seven principles of consumer choice

As Table 2.1 describes, there are seven principles underlying the post-Keynesian theory of consumer choice. Procedural rationality was discussed at length earlier. It is one of the presuppositions of heterodox economics. The great majority of consumer decisions are spontaneous and are the result of routine and habits, or based only on a few criteria. For instance, in choosing, say, a chair, colour preference may be insignificant in comparison to the quality of the leather that consumers demand. Households may not consider all possible options, except perhaps in the case of more important purchases. Indeed, non-compensatory decision criteria allow consumers to take quick decisions.

Moreover, consumers often entertain *thresholds*; this is the principle of the satiation of needs. Beyond a threshold, purchasing additional units of a given good brings no satisfaction. While this may resemble the neoclassical principle of decreasing marginal utility (the neoclassical non-saturation principle), it is actually very different. Indeed, the post-Keynesian principle of satiation exists at a positive price and finite income.

Table 2.1:   The seven principles of the post-Keynesian theory of choice

Procedural rationality (Simon)	Consumers will tend to follow habits, find shortcuts, use non-compensatory rules, satisfice (instead of maximize).
Satiable wants (Georgescu-Roegen)	Beyond a given threshold, the need is met, and more of one good will bring no additional satisfaction.
Separation of needs (Lancaster)	The consumer subdivides needs or expenditures into many categories, only loosely tied to one another.
Subordination of needs (Georgescu-Roegen)	Needs are often hierarchized, one need being subordinated to another.
Growth of needs (Georgescu-Roegen and Pasinetti)	Time and increases in income allow movement from one need to another within the hierarchy of needs.
Non-independence (Galbraith)	Needs are influenced by publicity, fashion, heroes, culture, family, friends ...
Heredity (Georgescu-Roegen)	Curent choices depend on the choices made in the past.

The separability of needs.   The next two principles are certainly the most important since they can have considerable repercussions. According to the principle of the separability of needs, needs or categories of consumer expenditures can be clearly distinguished from one another.

It would be an almost impossible task accurately to allocate our income to various consumer goods while taking into account the relative prices of all goods under consideration. Rather, to offset this complexity, consumers take a series of decisions that simplify and subdivide their task. For instance, they allocate specific budgets to various components, such as food, clothing, services, leisure, housing and transportation. Within each of these categories, they then evaluate various sub-categories or subgroups, independently of the others. Consequently, we can imagine a number of expenditure streams, each with a multitude of possibilities, each of which represents a subgroup of expenditures.

Changes in relative prices within a subgroup will not affect decisions relative to goods and services in another subgroup.

Changes in relative prices will only affect decisions regarding goods within the same subgroup. For instance, a decrease in the price of, say, shirts may affect the demand for trousers, but will not affect the demand for services or computers. Only a global or general increase in the price of all goods within a subgroup may then have an impact on monies allocated to other subgroups. For instance, an overall increase in the price of clothing may have an affect on expenditures on food.

In fact, empirical studies clearly show that the price elasticities for major subgroups are extremely weak (between −0.003 and −0.072 according to one such study) and cross-price elasticities close to zero (in fact, inferior to 0.02, 30 out of 36 times; see Eichner, 1987, ch. 7). In other words, substitution effects between subgroups are virtually nil. In fact, substitution effects, which are so central to neoclassical theory, are confirmed only when goods are similar to one another (fruit juices and sodas, for instance).

The subordination of needs.   Substitution effects can be weakened still further if we consider another important principle: the subordination of needs. This principle is in fact often associated with the pyramid of needs suggested by Abraham Maslow and his humanistic school of psychology (in order, physiological needs, then material, luxury, social and moral needs). The allocation of budgets is done on a hierarchical order: essential needs are first financed until they are satiated. If any income is left, then discretionary spending is allocated to other subgroups, in order of priority. It is in this sense that choices are considered to be lexicographic.

According to this principle, utility cannot be represented by a unique value; if utility exists, it should be considered rather as a vector where each component is linked to a need. This is what Georgescu-Roegen (1966) calls the principle of irreducibility, which we can also call the principle of incommensurability.

There is no possible arbitrage between goods that belong to different subgroups. There is no longer any possible substitution between these expenditure categories. Archimedes' axioms and the notion of gross substitution, so essential to neoclassical theory, no longer hold. The postulates that 'everything has a price' and that 'any good can be substituted for another', are unsubstantiated. The only possible substitution occurs within a subgroup.

Box 2.1: Post-Keynesians and ordering of a lexicographic nature

While post-Keynesians have never really developed their views on consumer choice in any systematic way, we can nonetheless find some interesting and coherent insights from a number of the better-known and more prolific post-Keynesians, such as Joan Robinson (1956), Luigi Pasinetti (1981, ch. 4), Edward Nell (1992, ch. 17), Alfred Eichner (1987, ch. 9) and Philip Arestis (1992, ch. 5). But the most interesting work to date has been carried out by Peter Earl (1983). In Lavoie (1992a, ch. 2), we can find a discussion of five of the seven principles described here, and we can also find a formal presentation of orderings of a lexicographic nature in Drakopoulos (1994).

If we had to formalize the principles of separability and sub-ordination of needs, many post-Keynesians would be tempted to adopt Kevin Lancaster's (1971) analysis of the characteristics of goods.

According to Lancaster, consumers are interested in the characteristics of a particular good, not the good itself. Each good offers a vector of characteristics; hence all goods taken together can be represented by a matrix of consumption. When the matrix is decomposable, it implies that a specific need can be attributed to each group of characteristics. This is the principle of separability, which is accepted even by some neoclassical authors.

From here, if we want to discuss the principle of subordination, we need to introduce orderings of a lexicographic nature, which suggest that we order and prioritize groups of characteristics. Lancaster (1971, p. 154) follows this approach, which he calls 'dominance', but he does not put much faith in it, whereas Ironmonger (1972), who proposed this approach concurrently, is much in favour of it.

Growth, dependence and heredity. Admitting that there does indeed exist a hierarchy of needs, how is this hierarchy organized? And how do we move from one need to another? The principles of growth, dependence and heredity help to explain these questions. The principle of growth stipulates that households will make their way up the pyramid of needs as their income grows. Income effects

---

Box 2.2: René Roy: first advocate of the post-Keynesian theory of consumer choice

In 1943, René Roy, professor at l'École des Ponts et Chaussées, and a colleague of Maurice Allais, published a remarkable article in *Econometrica*, entitled 'La hiérarchie des besoins et la notion de groupe en économie des choix' ['The hierarchy of needs and the concept of groups in consumer choice theory'], which he had submitted in 1940. In this paper, Roy develops many aspects of this alternative consumer theory, in particular the principles of satiation, separability and subordination, as the following extract shows.

These groups are conceived and could seemingly be established on the basis of the fact that, before consuming goods tied to the high end of the hierarchy of needs, all individuals first allocate their income to goods or services that are essential for survival in conditions imposed by their physical nature, the climate, the specific characteristics of their residence and social constraints. It is therefore possible to classify all goods and services in groups and to state that all consumers do not access a group of a given level until they have fully satisfied the needs that the groups at lower levels are meant to fulfill ...

In the final analysis, and with particular reference to consumer phenomena, we think that the concept of urgency in satisfying human needs tends to create a ranking scale of consumer goods such that they can be classified into groups, whereas the concept of taste is expressed within each group in terms of individual consumers' choice of articles meeting their personal preferences ...

Only within each group do relative prices, combined with individual tastes, have any effect on the demand for specific commodities, through the mechanism of substitution.

(Roy, 2005, pp. 50, 51, 54)

---

explain the evolution within the pyramid of needs. We assume that the top of the pyramid is characterized by moral needs, which includes environmental issues.

Moreover, how do we come to have the needs that we have? How do we know the needs we require? Choices and the evolution of needs are influenced by the society in which we live, by fashion trends and marketing campaigns. This is what Galbraith (1958) calls the dependence effect: consumers observe other members of society – the more notorious ones or those that they wish to emulate – and they try to imitate their consumption behaviour. The principle of the dependence of needs, also sometimes called the principle of non-independence, is also closely linked to conspicuous consumption. It emphasizes the fact that individuals often consume more to satisfy others than for themselves, as was demonstrated by Veblen, Bourdieu and others.

But there exists yet another kind of dependence effect, a more intrinsic one, which has been called the heredity principle. It is one of the better proven facts in experimental psychology. It explains that choices are not independent of the order in which they were made. Georgescu-Roegen argued that choices made out of habit are subject to this principle of heredity. The satisfaction that one derives from a particular experience depends, for instance, on past experiences, on the time in between these events, but also on the duration and intensity of past experiences. The heredity principle is the equivalent of historical time as applied to consumer choice theory: past choices will influence future choices. It is a kind of hysteresis effect: the current situation depends on the path taken in the past. The initial choice of, say, an X-Box, will eliminate the need to purchase a DVD player in the future.

Implications for economic theory and policy

The principle of irreducibility, which is the combination of the principles of separability and subordination, implies that goods cannot be treated in an identical fashion. In other words, there exists an asymmetry with respect to the impact of price changes on quantity demanded. For instance, any change in the price of a good belonging to a discretionary group (gadgets of some sort) will have no impact on the quantities demanded for a good associated with an essential need (such as bread). However, any change in the price of an essential good will have an effect on the quantity demanded for luxury goods or those deemed less essential.

The irreducibility principle in fact justifies certain state interventions, in particular controlling and subsidizing the prices of necessary goods that satisfy the essential needs of the population.

We could say the same about such policies as rent control or social housing. By lowering the price of these essential goods, more individuals are able to satisfy their priority needs.

Implications for environmental studies

Post-Keynesian consumption theory allows us to explain a frequently observed phenomenon in environmental studies. Authors using contingent valuation models try to estimate the amount of money that consumers would be willing to pay or to accept in compensation for a better or worse environment or conservation of wildlife. These authors have for years observed an incredible number of answers – bids – that are inconsistent with neoclassical theory and its indifference curves.

Many individuals answer that they would accept no compensation, while elsewhere in the questionnaire, they readily admit that they are concerned with environmental issues. Other respondents give answers involving ludicrously large amounts of money.

Yet, these answers make sense provided we accept that these consumers consider the environment to be a primary need, subject to a minimal income constraint. No possible amount of money is sufficient to compensate them for the deterioration of the environment; yet to express their feelings on the issue, they either go for zero bids or they bid for an almost infinite amount. These are protest bids (Spash and Hanley, 1995).

2.2 Oligopolistic markets and the objectives of firms

Characteristics of the post-Keynesian firm

The neoclassical theory of the firm is essentially pure fiction: it assumes a small firm facing diminishing returns, which maximizes profits in the short run in a perfectly competitive environment, producing a level of output where market price is equal to marginal cost. The firm remains afloat as long as the price is above the average variable cost. If demand increases, so do prices.

The post-Keynesian firm is of a rather different nature. It operates in the context of imperfect competition, more specifically in oligopolistic markets, where a few large firms, the megacorps, dominate a series of smaller firms.

Box 2.3: Jean Anouilh: a fine connoisseur of lexicographic choices

Jean Anouilh, author of a number of plays, is by any definition an accomplished analyst of human behaviour. In the following excerpt, he describes the discussion between Messerchmann, a rich industrialist, and Isabelle, a young, dazzling but poor dancer whom Mr Messerchmann would very much like to bribe so she can leave the castle, since she offends his daughter who is in love with the lord of the manor. Consider the following passage:

M: How much do you want to leave without seeing him again?

I: Nothing, Sir. I did not intend to see him again.

M: Miss, I don't like it when things are free.

I: Do free things worry you?

M: They seem priceless to me ... I find you very likeable and I am willing to be very generous to you. How much do you want?

I: Nothing, Sir.

M: It's too dear.

(Jean Anouilh (1972) [1951], *L'invitation au château*, Paris: Éditions de la Table Ronde (Folio), Paris, Act IV, pp. 325–8)

The text is an excellent example of lexicographic ordering. When Messerchmann asks Isabelle how much money she would be willing to accept to leave the castle, she says 'nothing'. This is a protest bid. Her departure cannot be bought, or if it could, the required amount of money would be infinite. Her preferences are lexicographic. Messerchmann is not fooled and understands this only too well. That is why when Isabelle answers that her willingness-to-accept price is zero – nothing – he interjects: 'It is too dear'!

Firms are also interdependent, since the decisions taken by one firm have consequences for other firms. This suggests that firms must take into consideration rival firms, including firms that may eventually enter the market. As such, strategy is a substantial com-

---

Box 2.4: Choices of a lexicographic nature within environmental economics

Assume individuals who must choose between the quality (or size) of forests and their own private consumption, f and y. We will assume that as long as their income is below y^*, they will prefer the bundle with the highest net income (their maximum consumption), irrespective of the size of the forest. However, for an equal net income, the individual prefers the bundle that has the biggest forest. We would then say that private consumption is the individual's first choice while the forest is his secondary choice. This is depicted in Figure 2.1 with horizontal quasi-indifference curves with an arrow. The higher the curve, the higher the level of satisfaction. But on any given horizontal curve, any rightward movement represents even more satisfaction.

But, for a net income equal or higher than y^*, the primary concern is the size of the forest, and the net income becomes the secondary concern. The quasi-indifference curves are now vertical. The more individuals find themselves to the right, the happier they are. They have become 'green' consumers. Hence, according to Figure 2.1, they would prefer the following situations: $A > C > B > D > E > G$.

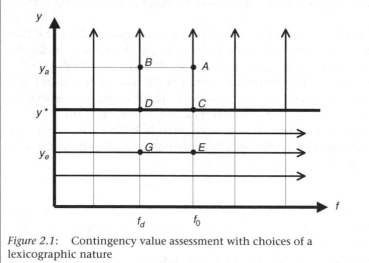

Figure 2.1:   Contingency value assessment with choices of a lexicographic nature

Box 2.4: Choices of a lexicographic nature within environmental economics – *cont'd*

Let us assume that an individual is at point A, surrounded by a forest of given size f_0, with an income y_a. Under these conditions what would this person be ready to pay to prevent the reduction of the forest? This amount is obviously $y_a - y^*$, since below y^* net income would become the primary concern. But this amount greatly underestimates the true value of the forest. If the forest was greatly reduced and green consumers now found themselves at point B, their satisfaction would be much less than if they were at point C. Moreover, what amount of money would sufficiently compensate each of them for allowing the disappearance of part of the forest? In fact, this amount would be indeterminate or infinite.

Consequently, in the case of those individuals for whom the forest has become the primary criterion for their lexicographic ordering, contingency evaluations do not adequately reflect a freely-agreed exchange, as should be the case in any market, even a hypothetical one. Rather, the proposed transaction resembles a ransom more than anything else. Yet, in any ransom situation, a person can never be indifferent between the value of the ransom paid and the value of the ransomed item or human. Neoclassical welfare theory is thus invalidated. Irrespective of the size by which the forest is reduced, the individual can only contribute $y_a - y^*$.

ponent of business. firms must plan ahead and adopt a strategy with an eye on the long term. This is particularly true of decisions regarding pricing, as is shown in Table 2.2, where various post-Keynesian taxonomies of pricing and market structures are outlined.

In this sense, prices are not determined by 'market forces' or by a fictitious and omniscient auctioneer. Prices are *set* by firms. If they are price takers, they will simply imitate the pricing policies of the leading firms in the industry. The latter then are the price leaders. These dominant or barometric firms must decide on the price that they will charge, and this price becomes the benchmark for the rest of the market. One thing is certain: prices do not clear markets; they are not set in an attempt to equalize supply and demand.

Table 2.2:   Different approaches to pricing and markets

Author	Post-Keynesian theory	Neoclassical theory
Kalecki (1971)	Cost-determined prices	Demand-determined prices
Means (1936)	Inflexible prices Administered prices	Flexible prices Market-clearing prices
Sawyer (1995)	Firm-determined prices Long-term strategic prices	Market-determined prices Short-term prices
Okun (1981)	Price maker Price-tag markets	Price taker Auction-market prices
Hicks (1974)	Fix-price markets	Flex-price markets
Chandler (1977)	Visible hand of management	Invisible hand of markets

Some post-Keynesians, such as Galbraith (1967), emphasize the divorce between owners and managers as one of the characteristics of the post-Keynesian firm. But like Robinson (1956, ch. 7), we assume rather that both owners and managers share the same goal: the long-run survival of the firm (except in abnormal circumstances, as was the case during the financial market euphoria of the 1990s). To achieve this, they will develop a number of strategies and objectives

One of the characteristics of the megacorp is their ownership of several factories or plants, which offer a variety of goods and services. Their average variable costs are roughly constant, as we will discuss below.

Power and growth

Many studies have shown that management has in fact multiple objectives. But to survive, firms must acquire the means to control their economic environment, for instance, by preventing the entry of new and rival firms in the industry, by developing their R&D, and by exercising control over suppliers, financiers, the future of the industry and government legislation. To exercise control, the firm must have power, which is the means by which its survival is guaranteed. Power also ensures that corporate management occupies a high place in the social hierarchy and retains the respect of peers.

But because power is a vague and many-sided concept, studies have shown that firms have multiple explicit intermediary objectives. But how do megacorps obtain power? A firm with impressive sales figures and a large market share has more power. Power is therefore linked to the size of the firm and to the share of the market it commands. To gain power and market share, firms must grow. Hence, growth is the means by which a firm acquires additional power. This implies that if we are to argue that firms actually do maximize something, we must conclude that they seek to maximize growth.

Among post-Keynesians, growth has always played an essential role. According to Robinson (1962, p. 38), 'the central mechanism of accumulation is the urge of firms to survive and to grow'. This is true for all time periods in capitalist societies, whether now, in Veblen's time 100 years ago, or in Galbraith's time 50 years ago.

For post-Keynesians, there is neither an optimal size of the firm, nor diminishing returns. Firms are constrained by their rates of growth, not by their absolute size.

Kalecki's principle of increasing risk

What can we say about profits then? What is their role in capitalism? The simple answer is that profits allow firms to grow by enabling them to borrow from both the financial markets and the banks. Moreover, undistributed profits (also called retained earnings) allow firms to finance a large part of their capital expenditures as well as internal research and development.

According to neoclassical theory, any entrepreneur can find funds to expand a business. All that is required is to demonstrate the seriousness and the future expected profitability of the projected investment. This sounds very much like the 'new economy' craze, with its internet and software start-ups, which lasted for a few years, becoming quickly overshadowed by the reality of lost illusions.

In the real world, however, firms face important financial constraints. The post-Keynesian theory of the firm rests firmly on Kalecki's (1971, ch. 9) principle of increasing risk, which is linked to the notion of fundamental uncertainty. The maximum amount of funds a firm can secure either from a bank or from financial markets depends on the sales of the firm, more specifically on its retained earnings, since lenders wish to limit their own risks. Hence, the funds lent to the firm will be a multiple of its current level of retained earnings. Moreover, genuine entrepreneurs (as opposed to crooks) will also want to limit the proportion of the borrowed funds, fearing the possibility of placing themselves in an illiquid or defaulting situation that may threaten the survival of the firm. This is the borrower's risk.

Profits thus enable firms to increase their capital, to ensure a healthy financial position, and to have access to bank credit or the commercial paper market. Profits are the solution to the financial requirements that constrain the growth-maximizing objective of the firm.

The expansion frontier

What is then the relationship between the profit rate and the growth rate pursued by a firm? Post-Keynesians, following Wood (1975), believe firms face essentially two constraints. On the one hand, there is a finance frontier, which combines each growth rate pursued by firms with the minimum profit rate required to finance this expansion, subject to Kalecki's principle of increasing risk. On the other hand, there is the expansion frontier, which for each growth rate relates the maximum profit rate firms can hope to reach. These frontiers must be thought of as constraints operating on firms and their long-term prospects.

The bell-shaped expansion frontier, as shown in Figure 2.2 below, suggests that the growth of an institution can carry both positive

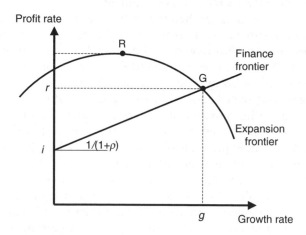

Figure 2.2:   Finance and expansion frontiers of a single firm

and negative effects. We assume that when rates of growth are weak, positive effects outweigh the negative effects. When firms invest a lot, they are better able to integrate the latest technologies and therefore reduce their costs of production and increase their profit rate. However, with ever faster growth, it becomes more difficult to familiarize employees with the philosophy and the management techniques of the firm. This is what we call the Penrose effect, so named after Edith Penrose (1959), a friend of Joan Robinson. Moreover, rapid growth often implies diversifying towards less familiar lines of products, engaging in important marketing expenses, or reducing profit margins. All of these are bound to reduce the maximum attainable profit rate, thus explaining the downward-sloping part of the expansion frontier.

The finance frontier

The finance frontier explains the internal and external financing opportunities of the firm. Investment can be financed internally (self-financed) or externally, through debt, either by borrowing from banks or turning to financial markets by issuing shares. We assume borrowed funds are a multiple, ρ, of retained earnings. Hence, assuming that firms make profits, P, and that i is the average rate of interest and dividend payments on capital, K, the following equation depicts the maximum value of investment:

$$I = (P - iK) + \rho(P - iK)$$

If we divide each side by K, we get I/K, the growth rate of the capital stock, g, and P/K, which is the profit rate on capital. Rearranging, we get the finance frontier (Marris, 1964; Sylos Labini, 1971), which defines the minimum profit rate, r, that a firm must get in order to grow at g, when the interest and the dividend rate are equal to i. All three variables can be expressed in nominal or in real terms, when deflated by the inflation rate. After some manipulation, the finance frontier is given by the following equation:

$$r = i + g/(1+ \rho)$$

When the two frontiers meet each other ...

The expansion and the finance frontiers are depicted in Figure 2.2. The intersection of these two frontiers, at point G, yields the maximum growth rate of the firm, as constrained by its competitive and financial environment. This point is different from R, which corresponds to the neoclassical solution and the maximization of the profit rate. Firms that suffer from X-inefficiencies, to use Harvey Leibenstein's (1978) expression, would be somewhere in between these two frontiers, which is the only attainable zone besides the frontier lines themselves.

If managers wish the firm to grow at a faster rate, that is, to displace point G to the right, there are two possibilities. First, management can try to push the expansion frontier upwards by cutting the costs of the firm relative to those of its competitors, or by developing new products that would give it a definitive advantage (a temporary monopoly) over its competitors. Second, firm management can hope for a downward displacement of the finance frontier, arising from a decrease in the interest and dividend rates, or resulting from the adoption of more relaxed debt and borrowing norms.

2.3　The shape of cost curves

Post-Keynesians generally adopt Leontief-type technologies of production. Coefficients of production, which are the link between the number of machines used and the number of workers, on the one hand, and the output of the firm, on the other, are fixed technical coefficients, as long as the firm produces below its practical capacity (defined below). Hence, post-Keynesians reject the traditional neoclassical production function (such as the Cobb-Douglas function), with its assumed substitutability between capital and labour.

Each firm usually has a number of physical plants, which are generally divided into a number of segments or assembly lines. The level of *practical* capacity is defined as the production capacity of a plant or plant segment, as measured by engineers, the so-called engineer-rated capacity (Eichner, 1976, p. 62). Each segment is designed to operate with a given number of workers and for a given number of hours. For instance, only a single employee works on a single computer at any one time. Even if some flexibility is possible, bureaucratic rules and regulations, such as collective bargaining agreements, as well as customs and habits, dictate the number of employees on each machine. Fixed technical coefficients are the best description of the likely production conditions in the short period.

Stylized facts

We can draw from the above the following four stylized facts, which are at the core of the post-Keynesian theory of the firm (Eichner and Kregel, 1975):

- The unit direct costs and marginal costs of a plant are approximately constant, up to practical capacity as defined by engineers.
- The unit cost of a product is generally decreasing until the firm reaches its practical capacity (see Box 2.5 below).
- It is possible to produce beyond practical capacity, but at increasing marginal costs.
- The sum of all practical or engineer-rated capacities is what we call the full capacity of a firm (q_{fc}); firms usually operate below their full capacity. In this sense, firms will operate, except under exceptional cases, where average production costs are constant.

When historical time and technical progress are taken into account, it must then be conceded that the unit direct cost is higher in an old plant than in a more recent plant producing an identical product. In this sense, it is impossible to claim that the unit direct cost across all plants of a single firm is absolutely constant. We will, however, ignore this complication and assume that a firm will often spread the production of its products across all plants, by considering not only the production cost but also the costs of transportation and delivery.

Excess capacity

Firms generally operate below the level of full capacity, q_{fc}, as shown in Figure 2.3. In fact, firms usually operate at anywhere from 70 per cent to 85 per cent of capacity. This stylized fact has been confirmed by numerous studies undertaken by statistical agencies or forecasting firms, as well as by researchers and specialists who found that firms consider 'normal' or 'standard' capacity utilization rates to be around 80 per cent. But why don't firms attempt to produce nearer to full capacity rates, that is at 100 per cent? After all, this is where unit costs would be at their lowest, as can be seen from Figure 2.3. Why do they prefer producing with some capacity reserves?

Box 2.5: Direct costs, overhead costs and unit costs

British authors often refer to *direct costs* or *prime costs*, and hence to a *unit direct cost* which we can write as *UDC*. These include wages, the cost of raw materials and intermediate goods directly linked to the making of the product. As long as they are constant, unit direct costs and marginal costs are equal. In fact, we can claim that unit direct costs are nearly identical to the average variable costs found in traditional microeconomics.

To get the *unit cost*, denoted *UC*, we need to take into account the general shop and enterprise expenditures. These are often called the *overhead costs* or *indirect costs*. They include costs linked to the supervision of the production process, as well as administrative and other possible costs related to the manufacturing of the product, such as the costs incurred to bring the product to its purchasers. The *unit cost* is thus the sum of the *unit direct cost* and the *unit overhead cost*. It decreases up to full capacity (Andrews, 1949).

The unit cost is similar to the average total cost that is found in traditional microeconomics (which is the sum of the average variable cost and the average fixed cost). Yet, contrary to average total cost, the unit cost does not include normal profits per unit produced, which are supposed to cover at the very least the amortization of fixed capital.

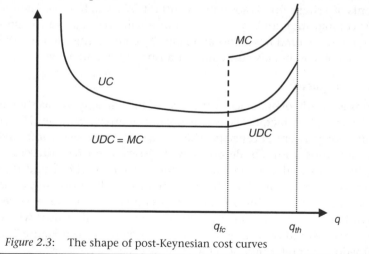

Figure 2.3:   The shape of post-Keynesian cost curves

Apart from a possible explanation based on the concept of indivisibility (an optimal plant may be too large for the existing market), fundamental uncertainty once again offers us the best possible explanation. Planned excess capacity for firms plays a role which resembles that of monetary liquidity for individual agents. Households hold money balances or have access to credit lines so that they can absorb any unexpected fluctuation in their cash flows; similarly firms cannot predict with certainty what demand will be in the future. Firms must give themselves some production elbow-room to meet any unexpected change in demand or in its composition. Hence, having temporarily inoperative plants or segments of plants allows firms to adapt supply to changing demand conditions much more easily (Steindl, 1952, ch. 1).

This flexibility is also acquired through inventories. The problem, however, is that inventories can only be used once, as a response to an unforeseen boost in demand. Other sources of flexibility are overtime work, paid at a higher wage, and the addition of another work shift. Both of these will bring production beyond practical capacity, up to the level of theoretical capacity, q_{th}. But under such conditions, machines are subject to more frequent breakdowns – which can be costly; this will interrupt production and ultimately result in the firm losing some of its customers.

If demand is systematically greater than expected, and if it grows more rapidly and continuously, firms might be unable to keep pace with it in the medium run. The construction of additional plants and factories, as well as that of the required machines and equipment, takes time. Without planned excess capacity, increased demand may be met by foreign firms or by firms producing closely-related merchandise. Reserve capacity is thus part of the overall strategy of the firm in preventing rival firms from entering the market.

Firms therefore prefer to produce with excess capacity, enabling better response to spurts in demand for specific products and allowing them better to meet their clients' needs. Firms know that their customers, in capitalist countries, have no patience for delivery lags and delays. If customers cannot buy a specific product now, they will probably buy a slightly different product manufactured by a rival firm. Yet, firms want to preserve their market share; it is a fundamental objective of any firm that wishes to survive. This is why firms prefer to hold reserve capacity, even if it seems, at first glance, somewhat inefficient.

Box 2.6: Questions regarding capacity utilization

Statistics Canada, the Canadian national statistical agency, carries out an annual survey (the *Capital and Repair Expenditures Survey*) in which they ask 7000 companies questions regarding their capacity utilization rates (there is a similar annual survey done through the US Census Bureau, entitled *Survey of Plant Capacity Utilization*). In surveying these firms, they ask the following question: 'For [2006], this plant has been operating at which percentage of its capacity?' The survey specifies that 'Capacity is defined as maximum production attainable under normal conditions', by taking into account regular holidays. Statistics Canada offers two examples.

Plant 'A' normally operates one shift a day, five days a week and given this operation pattern, capacity production is 150 units of product for the month. In that month, actual production was 125 units. The capacity use rate for plant 'A' is (125/150) * 100 = 83%.

Now suppose that plant 'A' had to open for a shift on Saturdays to satisfy an abnormal surge in demand for its product. Given this plant's normal operation schedule, capacity production remains at 150 units. Actual production has grown to 160 units, so capacity use would be (160/150) * 100 = 107%.

2.4 Price setting

All post-Keynesian models rely on *cost-plus pricing*. In order to arrive at a specific price, the office in charge of setting prices begins by determining a unit cost, to which it adds a costing margin (the expression 'profit' margin should best be kept to measure the actual, realized, or ex post margin, which in the real world may turn out to be different from the ex ante costing margin). This price is always determined in advance, well before products hit their market (Brunner, 1975). We can therefore say that the price is 'administered', as Means (1936) would put it. Of course there is interdependence between the products. The price of intermediate goods sold by one firm to other firms in a different sector becomes a cost for these firms (this interdependence is a crucial element in Sraffian models).

Mark-up pricing

The simplest post-Keynesian theory of price formation is the Kaleckian theory of mark-up pricing. It is in fact the oldest price-setting method, which is still used today by a number of small and medium enterprises, since it involves very little accounting expertise. Given its simplicity, it is also the version most frequently used in post-Keynesian macroeconomic models.

According to this approach, prices depend on unit direct costs. A gross costing margin – covering all general costs and other salaries, as well as anticipated profits – is then added to the unit direct cost, thus arriving at the price of the product.

Since unit direct costs are roughly constant, whatever the level of production (as long as it is below full capacity), it follows that the accounting involved in this method of determining prices does not need to be sophisticated.

Normal-cost pricing

The method that seems the most realistic and the one most commonly found among large firms is what is called *normal pricing* or *normal-cost pricing*. This approach takes into consideration recent developments in accounting practices, which allow firms easily to assign a part of the general costs of production to each manufactured product. According to Frederic Lee (1998), large firms have been using normal-cost pricing, as opposed to simple mark-up approaches, since at least the 1920s. Normal-cost methods are also known as *full-cost pricing* and were first explored by Hall and Hitch (1939) in their Oxford study on the behaviour of firms.

Under normal-cost pricing, firms must first calculate a *normal* unit cost to which they then add a net costing margin covering profits.

Normal unit costs include all direct and indirect (overhead) costs, which can be attributed to the product in question, but they are calculated for a normal or standard level of production, which is not the same as the estimated or expected level of production for that period. Rather the normal level is a conventional level of production, fixed by the firm following standards and norms of the corporation or those of the industry, given its habits or the industry's or manufacturers' conventions. The normal level of production is usually the product of full capacity and of the normal (or standard) rate of capacity utilization.

The advantage of this approach is that firms do not need to know their unit costs for all levels of production. Rather, they only need to know their unit cost for a single level of production, that corresponding to the normal rate of capacity utilization. This is normal-cost pricing. This normal unit cost is independent of changes in demand.

Target-return pricing

Numerous studies have confirmed that both large and medium-sized firms now prefer to use a method where they target a rate of return. As discussed by Lanzillotti (1958) in his Brookings Institution studies, target-return pricing is a more specific version of normal-cost pricing. As in the case of normal costs, a net costing margin is added to normal unit costs. This net margin includes a target rate of return on the capital of the firm, when sales are just equal to the production resulting from a normal level of capacity utilization. This method is surely the most sophisticated of all cost-plus pricing methods, because accountants must have a proper assessment of the value of the capital used by the firm.

Target-return pricing is very close to the Sraffian theory of prices of production used in multisectoral models. In fact, the targeted rate of return is equivalent to the normal profit rate used in the theory of prices of production. In Sraffian models, the normal profit rate is the same in all industries or sectors, as is the wage rate of labour. With target-return pricing, however, the profit rate and the wage rate may be different from one sector to another. We can thus conclude that the Sraffian model is the idealized version of a multisectoral model based on target-return pricing.

Box 2.7: The formalization of cost-plus pricing procedures

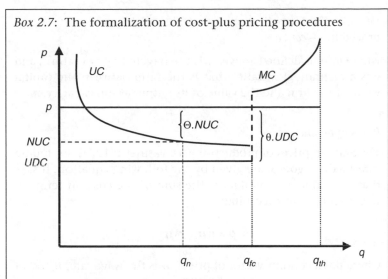

Figure 2.4:   The setting of normal prices

We can formalize the various cost-plus pricing procedures in the following way:

Mark-up pricing

$$p = (1+\theta)(UDC)$$

UDC is unit direct costs (average variable costs), θ is the gross costing margin.

Normal-cost pricing

$$p = (1 + \Theta)(NUC)$$

Θ is the net costing margin, whereas NUC is the normal unit cost (the normal average total cost), calculated at a standard or normal level of production, $q_n = u_n q_{fc}$, where u_n is the standard or normal rate of utilization of full capacity, q_{fc}.

Target-return pricing

The equation is the same as normal-cost pricing, but the value of the net costing margin, Θ, is specifically defined to be:

$$\Theta = r_n v / (u_n - r_n v)$$

Box 2.7: The formalization of cost-plus pricing
procedures – *cont'd*

where u_n is as defined above; r_n is the targeted rate of return; and
v is a technological ratio, that is the ratio between the capital
value of the firm and the value of its output at full capacity, q_{fc}.

Prices of production

The Sraffian prices of production (see Pasinetti, 1977), excluding
intermediate goods, are given by the following equation. It says
that the value of a product is the sum of the costs in terms of
wages and profits on capital:

$$p = wn + rMp$$

where p is a column-vector of prices, w is the wage rate, n and M
are a vector and a matrix of technical coefficients representing
respectively labour per unit of output and the amounts of each
kind of machines per unit of output. Finally, r is the uniform
profit rate.

We can re-write the above equation:

$$p = wn \, [I - rM]^{-1}$$

This equation is very similar to target-return pricing in the case
of the simple firm. By integrating the value of Θ in the normal-
cost pricing equation, and assuming that direct costs are wages
per unit of production, we get:

$$p = u_n wn \, (u_n - r_n v)^{-1}$$

The last two equations are essentially identical, once we note
that Sraffians assume that the standard rate of capacity utilization, u_n, is unity. In addition the Sraffian uniform profit rate
r is what Sraffians also call the normal profit rate, which is no
different from the target rate of return r_n of the normal-cost
pricing procedures.

Box 2.7: The formalization of cost-plus pricing procedures – *cont'd*

The remaining question now is to explain how – and indeed if – these prices of production ever come about (with or without a unique rate of return). This is the issue of the gravitation around prices of production or that of the convergence towards prices of production.

Two dominant approaches have been proposed. One is based on the so-called cross-dual dynamics, where prices react to discrepancies between quantities supplied and demanded, as advocated by most Sraffians and Marxists (Duménil and Lévy, 1993). The second approach relies on some kind of normal-cost pricing procedure, where cost changes get translated into price changes. This last approach is proposed by other Sraffians, such as Boggio (1980), and is closer to the Kaleckian stream.

2.5 The determinants of the costing margin

Are cost-based prices entirely realistic?

Some economists have questioned the validity of cost-plus pricing, perhaps because it seems to undermine the virtues of capitalism and its underlying faith in competition between firms. After all, it seems difficult to believe that all firms can always simply decide to change their prices whenever their unit costs change.

Of course, this is not the case. We must understand that prices are a function of *normal* unit costs. While in the medium run normal unit costs are closely linked to realized unit costs, in the short run they may diverge significantly, irrespective of the causes behind the changes in the realized unit costs. When costs change, the chances are that these changes will imply a modification of the costing margin rather than a change in the price. It all depends on the kind of strategies being pursued by the firm at any point in time. In fact, studies done by Coutts et al. (1978) and by Sylos Labini (1971) show that firms only gradually recover increases in their unit costs.

The same phenomenon occurs within the context of contemporary global markets. In industries where competition is particularly fierce, or in markets where imported products are only a small component, foreign firms fix their prices on the basis of domestic prices. These companies either absorb losses or post windfall profits when exchange rates fluctuate. On the other hand, in industries where foreign firms dominate, the latter tend to pass over to foreign customers their domestic cost increases as well as the effects of changes in exchange rates – the so-called passthrough effects (Bloch and Olive, 1995).

Price leaders and price takers

This whole discussion leads us to distinguish between the price leader, which sets prices, and the price taker, which follows the lead of the price leader. The cost-plus approach explains how prices depend essentially on direct unit costs or normal unit costs, both assumed to be constant in the short run, whatever the changes in demand. But, as Kalecki (1971) argued, firms set their prices on the basis of some measure of unit cost, but they also take into account the prices set by other firms. In fact, in both competitive and oligopolistic surroundings, all firms will tend to set the same price for a given product.

Mark-up and normal-cost pricing procedures explain how price leaders – those firms that either dominate the market or serve as leader – set their own prices. Smaller firms, or those considered to be price takers, may well adopt the same procedures, but they also have to consider the prices set by their price leaders. This helps to explain why foreign firms may or may not pass over higher costs, depending on whether they are price leaders or price takers on foreign markets.

Less efficient firms face higher unit costs. As such, they will be unable to set costing margins in ways that will generate a normal target rate of return. They will have to put forward competitive prices, similar to those of their rivals. In the short run, they will thus be able to maintain their market share and respond to any sudden increase in demand. But in the medium and long run, market forces will take their toll, unless the firm is somehow able to modify its product and reduce its unit costs. Only then will the less efficient price taker be able to impose normal costing margins.

Otherwise, competition will impose financial constraints on inefficient firms by limiting their ability to pursue investments in their productive capacity or in research and development (Steindl,

1952; Kaldor, 1985, p. 47). The intersection of the expansion frontier and of the financial constraint will force those high-cost firms to reduce their growth rate, thus diminishing their market share and, ultimately, leading to their disappearance.

Target-return pricing and its determinants

What determines the net costing margin? Its determinants were identified earlier in Box 2.7 dealing with the formalization of cost-plus pricing methods: net costing margins are inversely proportional to the standard rate of capacity utilization, and proportional to the target rate of return and the capital to capacity ratio (or to the *incremental* capital to capacity ratio, if management is only concerned with the profitability of the most recent investments). But if we assume that the standard utilization rate depends on corporate or industry norms, and that the capital to capacity ratio depends on issues related to engineering, then ultimately the net costing margin depends on the target rate of return. But then what are the determinants of the target rate of return? In other words, what determines the normal profit rate? Four determinants may be identified (Table 2.3).

According to the Marxist tradition, the normal profit rate depends on class struggle, and on the entrepreneurs' bargaining power relative to that of workers (labour laws, the unemployment rate and so on). According to Kaleckians, however, in addition to class struggle, the gross costing margin, and thus the normal profit rate, will depend on the degree of monopoly of the firm, in particular the degree of concentration and the ability of firms to prevent the entry of new competitors.

In the post-Keynesian tradition, especially in the old growth models of Robinson (1956) and Kaldor (1956), there is a proportional relationship between the growth rate of the economy and the macroeconomic profit rate. The same relationship is to be found in the works of Pasinetti (1981, 1993), based on the concept of a 'natural' economy, which assigns to each vertically integrated sector a profit rate equal to the growth rate of the sector.

Following Steindl (1952, p. 51) and Lanzillotti (1958), numerous post-Keynesians, such as Eichner (1987) and Wood (1975), have argued in favour of a similar relationship, establishing a microeconomic link between the trend growth rate of a firm and its target rate of return or net costing margin.

Table 2.3:   The various determinants of the target rate of return or of the normal profit rate

Tradition	Determinants
Marxist	Class struggle
Kaleckian	The degree of concentration and the ability to prevent the entry of potential rivals
Cambridge	The growth rate of capital
Sraffian	The rate of interest set by the central bank

More recently, Sraffian authors have offered a fourth possibility: the normal profit rate depends on the trend rate of interest, historically realized or expected in the future (Pivetti, 1985; Panico, 1988). In other words, during a period of high real interest rates imposed by the central bank, there exists a higher real target rate of return. By the way, some post-Keynesians, such as Kaldor and Harrod, have endorsed such a view. For these authors, interest payments should be considered on the same level as all other costs, and firms will try to pass these on to consumers.

Are these various determinants compatible?

Given the various determinants discussed above, which explanation of the target rate of return is the right one? The answer, I think, is that all these approaches offer some valid suggestions. In fact, they can all be shown to be consistent with the analysis of the expansion and finance frontiers presented earlier. For instance, a decrease in the monopoly power of a firm or a decrease in the bargaining power of entrepreneurs relative to that of workers can be represented by a downward shift of the expansion frontier, and hence by a fall in the normal profit rate, for a given growth rate.

For those firms that attempt to maximize their growth rate, the target rate of return that is incorporated in their prices is the one that is determined by the intersection of both frontiers. The finance frontier may thus be rewritten as:

$$r_n = i_n + g_s/(1+\rho)$$

The target rate of return, r_n, will be high whenever the trend rate of interest, i_n, and the trend growth rate – the secular growth rate g_s – of the firm or the industry are high.

As we can see, the use of the finance and expansion frontiers allows us to bridge the various heterodox approaches. As such, a cyclical increase in demand could provoke an increase in the costing margin if it gets translated into an increase in the target rate of return. Otherwise, changes in demand should not lead to changes in the costing margin, as has been shown in numerous studies.

2.6 Consequences for macroeconomic theory

The above discussion carries obvious implications for the theory of inflation. Whereas neoclassical economists believe that increases in aggregate demand necessarily lead to increases in costs and prices, as a result of diminishing returns, post-Keynesians reject this approach outright. With the exception of a few sectors, such as agriculture and raw materials, an increase in demand will neither lead to an increase in unit costs nor to an increase in prices. This explains why post-Keynesians advocate the use of raw material buffer stocks (Kaldor, 1976). As a result, inflation would not be a 'natural' phenomenon, but would depend rather on institutional and sociological factors, which could be managed.

3
A Macroeconomic Monetary Circuit

A necessary first step in understanding macroeconomics is a full discussion of monetary and financial issues. The principle of effective demand which is one of the two essential features of post-Keynesian economics – that is, the causality that runs from investment to saving – is best understood within the context of a macroeconomic explanation of the monetary circuit. This is why it is preferable to start with the monetary dimension of macroeconomics before we proceed to an explanation of employment and growth.

Post-Keynesian monetary theory has a long tradition going back to the writings of classical authors such as John Fullarton and Thomas Tooke in the 1830s and 1840s – the so-called 'banking school' (Panico, 1988; Wray, 1990). These authors objected to the currency school and the quantity theory of money upon which monetarism and textbook neoclassical macroeconomics are based. The banking school presented alternative views, among which was the concept of money endogeneity. Ironically, the endogenous view of money, which contrasts with the exogenous view of the quantity theory of money, was pursued in the early twentieth century by authors from the Austrian tradition, among them Ludwig von Mises, Joseph Schumpeter and Friedrich Hayek, as well as their predecessor, Swedish author Knut Wicksell (Bellofiore, 2005). Some famous post-Keynesian Cambridge authors, notably Kaldor and Kahn, who did develop an alternative monetary theory, were exposed early on to these heterodox views, the former having met Hayek when he was a student at LSE and the latter having been the translator of Wicksell.

The rejection of the quantity theory of money and the adoption of money endogeneity were always very strong in continental Europe, most notably in France, Italy and Germany, even in the heyday of monetarism. From here emerged a monetary school of thought, known as the theory of the circuit and monetary circulation – inspired by Keynes's *Treatise on Money* (1930) rather than his *General Theory* (1936) – which turned out to have very close links with post-Keynesian theory, as shown in two books emphasizing these linkages (Deleplace and Nell, 1996; Rochon and Rossi, 2003).

The most obvious point of differentiation between the modern exponents of the quantity theory of money and their opponents is expressed in the following quote, taken from an article, first published in 1962, by an early leader of the circuit school:

> There are two opposing viewpoints concerning the relationship between the supply of and the demand for money. On the one hand – for the Quantity theorists and Keynes – the quantity of money is believed to be fixed *independently* by the banking system ... The opposing view – held by the Banking school and Wicksell – is that the banks set not a quantity but *a price*. The banking system fixes a rate (or a set of rates) for the money market and then lends however much borrowers ask for, provided that they can offer satisfactory collaterals.
>
> (Le Bourva, 1992, p. 449)

The 'new consensus' and post-Keynesian theory

In the late 1950s, just when circuit theorists claimed that the banking school view was about to take over and the quantity theory of money was no longer tenable, the popularity of the latter soared to incredible heights with the advent of Friedman's monetarism. Only recently have we witnessed a reverse trend, with some post-Keynesian monetary views slowly being incorporated into the more recent incarnation of the new Keynesian approach, the so-called 'new monetary consensus' that is advocated by most central bankers. In fact, in the United States, there are examples of a few textbooks where Wicksellian views are making their way (J.B. Taylor, 2004; Cecchetti, 2006).

One of the more fundamental differences between the 'new consensus' and the post-Keynesian vision is that post-Keynesians categorically reject the Wicksellian theory of loanable funds which is still accepted by most new Keynesian economists. According to this theory, the rate of interest, in a moneyless world, is the price that equates loanable funds and real investment, that is, the rate that makes consistent preferences for the present and the productivity of capital. This is the *natural* rate of interest. The role of the central bank then is simply to ensure the equality between the monetary rate of interest prevailing on markets and the real rate of interest that would exist in a fictional world without money – the natural rate of interest. When market rates (in real terms) are set below the natural rate, inflation ensues. Post-Keynesians, however, strongly reject the existence of this natural rate (Rogers, 1989; Smithin, 2003).

But there exists yet another difference between the 'new consensus' and post-Keynesian theory. While the majority of new

Table 3.1: Characteristics of money in post-Keynesian and neoclassical economics

Characteristics	Post-Keynesian approach	Neoclassical approach
Money ...	must have a counterpart	falls from a helicopter
Money is ...	a flow and a stock	a stock
Money enters the economy ...	through production	with exchange
The supply of money is ...	endogenous	exogenous
Causality	Credits create deposits	Reserves create deposits
Interest rates ...	are distributive variables	are the result of market forces
The base rate of interest ...	is set by the central bank	is influenced by markets
A restrictive monetary policy ...	has negative effects in both the short and the long run	only has negative effects in the short run
The natural rate of interest ...	has multiple values or does not exist	is unique
Credit rationing is due to ...	a lack of confidence	asymmetric information

Keynesians believe that restrictive monetary policies, the aim of which is to reduce inflation to its target level, have no long-run effect on economic growth, post-Keynesians beg to differ. In fact, post-Keynesians believe that restrictive monetary policies have a negative impact on output, both in the short and the long run (see Table 3.1).

3.1 Main characteristics of post-Keynesian monetary analysis

Reverse causation

The cornerstone of post-Keynesian monetary analysis is its theory of endogenous money, where the supply of money cannot be set arbitrarily by the central bank: it is determined by the demand for bank credit (loans) and the public's preferences. For post-Keynesians, the supply of money is not independent of the needs of the economy: 'loans create deposits'.

Accordingly, the causality between loans and deposits is reversed. There is no need for banks to have access to prior deposits in order to extend loans. The creation of loans, and hence of monetary deposits (money), is done *ex nihilo*, without any previous need for gold or reserves. All that is required, as pointed out by Le Bourva (above), is a credible borrower, with appropriate collateral (Heinsohn and Steiger, 2000).

Moreover, the creation of this credit-money is not the result of excess reserves held by private banks. In this case, causality is also reversed. For post-Keynesians, banks first extend loans, creating deposits in the process. Then, if bank customers request bank notes (cash or currency), banks can get them directly from the central bank. Banks also obtain their required reserves, dictated by law, from the central bank (Moore, 1988).

High-powered money (reserves and currency), just like bank money (money deposits), is endogenous and demand-determined. It cannot be imposed arbitrarily by the central bank. In fact, the volume of high-powered money is directly related to the supply of bank loans and bank money through the *credit divisor*. Bank money is not a multiple of high-powered money, as claimed by neoclassical theorists; rather high-powered money is a quotient of the quantity of bank money.

The reversed causation suggested here is also at the root of two additional reversed causalities in post-Keynesian theory, which are particularly important. First, as already pointed out, it is investment undertaken by firms that creates saving. Investment requires neither prior saving nor a source of prior deposits. As long as the resources of a national economy are not fully utilized, the financing of economic activity depends only on the credibility of the borrower and on existing financial norms. The scarcity of finance is purely based on a norm – a convention (Parguez, 2001).

Second, inflation is not caused by an excessive rate of growth in the money supply. If anything, the causality is also reversed. The growth rate of prices and output instead cause the stock of money to increase. The inflation rate is explained through other causes.

Overdraft and asset-based economies

When discussing monetary theory, it is important to keep in mind the relevant institutional context. Indeed there are some important differences between Anglo-Saxon financial systems and those of the rest of the world, most notably in continental Europe and Asia, although it may be claimed that some of these differences are vanishing with the advent of globalization. Indeed these differences help to explain why monetarism with its exogenous stock of money never really took hold of monetary textbooks in continental Europe.

The most crucial differences may be associated with what Hicks (1974) has called 'overdraft economies' – which concern continental Europe and Asia – and 'auto-economies', although it might be best to refer to the latter as 'asset-based' financial systems – which would pertain to the Anglo-Saxon world.

In overdraft economies money is said to be endogenous, and commercial banks are indebted towards the central bank. In the case of asset-based economies, however, it is often argued that money is exogenous and under the control of the central bank. While this dichotomy may adequately reflect different institutional characteristics of central banks in various countries, it has no theoretical consequences. In other words, the distinction carries little relevance as to whether money is endogenous or not. Post-Keynesians believe that money is endogenous regardless of the specific institutional make-up. This suggests therefore that all modern financial systems operate under a similar context: that of the reversed causation discussed above. While the relevance of reversed causation may be more obvious in the context of overdraft financial systems, it is no less valid within asset-based economies.

Exogenous interest rates

In a modern economy, there exist a number of financial assets, each with its own rate of return. For post-Keynesians, at least one of these rates is under the direct control of the central bank and represents a reference point for financial markets around which all other rates, at least other short-run rates, will tend to gravitate. While there are a number of expressions for this rate – such as the key rate, official rate, the key policy rate or the operating target – I prefer to call it the 'benchmark rate' since it is effectively a benchmark for other interest rates on the short-term money market.

At one time, the benchmark rate was the rate at which the central bank lent to commercial banks (the 'bank rate' in Canada, for instance, or the 'discount window rate' in the USA). At other times, especially in countries where open market operations were an important component of monetary policy, the benchmark rate was the yield rate on short-term government securities (one to three month Treasury bills, for example). However, today, in most countries, the benchmark rate is related to the interbank (or overnight) rate – the rate at which commercial banks lend and borrow funds to and from one another in the overnight market, also called the federal funds rate in the USA.

The benchmark rate is the *target* overnight rate – the overnight rate that the central bank would like to see being realized. In Canada, this is the 'target for the overnight rate'; in the USA, it is the 'target for the federal funds rate'; in the UK, the 'two-week repo rate' set by the Bank of England; and in euroland, it is 'the main refinancing operations minimum bid rate', as set by the European Central Bank.

Under normal circumstances, a central bank that targets its benchmark rate at, say, 3 per cent, will be able to hit that target on a daily basis with very little error: the benchmark rate may end up at 2.99 per cent or at 3.01 per cent, for instance, deviating only very slightly from the target. This is the case notably in Canada and in Australia. In other cases, however, the central bank may not hit its target with as much accuracy, owing in part to the fact that the central bank cannot know with perfect certainty the exact amount of reserves that are in the system. In addition, the demand for reserves by commercial banks may change from one day to another. This is particularly the case of the European and American monetary systems. Nevertheless, the average spread between the benchmark rate (the target) and the actual federal funds rate in the USA is only 7 basis points.

As stated above, the interbank or overnight rate is the rate at which banks lend or borrow high-powered money to and from one another (over say, one, two, or even seven days). This rate is obviously very close to the repo rate, that is the rate at which banks and other financial market participants, including the central bank, borrow and lend Treasury bills (or other claims) from and to one another (for one, two or seven days). In the USA, the Federal Reserve intervenes on the repo market to either add or withdraw reserves in order to hit the target federal funds rate.

This mechanism is a powerful one: the central bank can always, with more or less accuracy, push overnight rates towards its target benchmark rate. Of course, markets are well aware of the ability of the central banks to hit their target rate. Hence, when the central bank decides to change its benchmark rate (for example, when it decides to raise it by 25 basis points), it does not even have to intervene and modify the supply of liquid balances: the central bank need only announce a new target and all other short-term interest rates immediately adjust. This is the best example of the exogeneity of the rate of interest.

3.2   The relationship between commercial banks and the central bank

High-powered money consists of banknotes supplied by the central bank, as well as bank deposits held by commercial banks at the central bank – the reserves and the clearing or settlement balances of commercial banks. For many post-Keynesians, at least for those that we call 'horizontalists', such as Kaldor (1982), Basil Moore (1988) and Louis-Philippe Rochon (1999), the central bank always stands ready to supply high-powered money on demand to the commercial banking system. High-powered money is perfectly endogenous, and can be depicted as a horizontal supply curve of money in a diagram with the interest rate on the vertical axis. With respect to banknotes, it is clear that their supply cannot be anything but endogenous. It is certainly difficult to imagine consumers unable to withdraw money from their bank accounts or from ATMs. Of course, this could perhaps happen under very stringent conditions, as was the case in Argentina in 2002, but it remains clearly a rare exception to the rule. This being said, discussion over the endogenous nature of high-powered money must therefore concentrate on the role of reserves.

The case of overdraft economies

The endogenous nature of high-powered money appears nearly obvious within the context of overdraft economies. In such economies, commercial banks face no constraints in borrowing banknotes or reserves from the central bank, as needs arise. This was particularly the case in France, and is still the case under the current euro system.

This situation is illustrated in Figure 3.1, which represents the balance sheet of the central bank and that of the banking system as a whole. The cardinal rule of balance sheets is that they must always be in equilibrium. This means, for instance, that if the reserves of the banking system increase, this change must be compensated by either a reduction in another asset of the banking system, or an increase in its liabilities. Similarly, if commercial banks increase their reserves with the central bank, thereby increasing the liabilities of the central bank, then the central bank must either decrease another of its liabilities by the same amount, or increase its assets.

In the case of an overdraft economy, commercial banks hold virtually no government securities. As a result, commercial banks can only obtain additional reserves by borrowing them from the central bank. We can conclude by saying that in an overdraft economy, an increase in reserves that arises from an increase in bank loans and bank deposits is made good by the necessary willingness of the central bank to provide advances to the commercial banking system.

Asset-based economies

Given the above, can we draw the same conclusions for Anglo-Saxon countries, which operate under a different institutional setting?

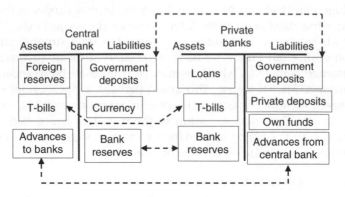

Figure 3.1:   Simplified balance sheets: the central bank and the banking system

In these asset-based economies, one of the more striking differences is that commercial banks appear to borrow very little – and in some cases not at all – from the central bank. How can we reconcile this with the statement made in section 3.1 of this chapter, where we claimed that the institutional setting of the financial system does not matter for our discussion of endogenous money?

Two answers can be given, both depicted in Figure 3.1. First, we can argue that commercial banks sell Treasury bills directly to the central bank in order to obtain reserves. This is the well-known case of 'open-market operations', illustrated in many textbooks.

Today, such operations take the form of repos or reverse repos, where the central bank does not buy securities outright, holding on to them for an indefinite period of time. Rather, the central bank agrees to purchase claims only on the condition that banks will repurchase them on the next day or in the very near future. Yet, once we consider the nature of these transactions, repo operations turn out to be a small variant of standard central bank advances within an overdraft financial system. With repos, central banks agree to lend reserves for a day, with Treasury bills or other claims acting as collateral.

The second answer to our puzzle is that the central bank may decide to move the government bank deposits between the central bank and the commercial banks – which is also practised in overdraft economies. When the central bank decides to move government deposits to a commercial bank, it credits the account of that bank. In effect, the central bank creates reserves.

This practice is increasingly used by central banks. It gives great flexibility in neutralizing any movement in reserves resulting from government expenditures or the payment of taxes. For instance, when the government spends, it essentially draws down its account at the central bank and transfers high-powered money to the account of the recipient at a commercial bank. Reserves are created in the process. The same happens, although in reverse, when households pay their taxes (with a cheque). In this case, money balances are transferred from a household's banking account to the account of the government at the central bank. Hence, bank reserves are reduced. In both of these situations, the central bank can effectively neutralize the effects on reserves by moving government deposits in the opposite direction.

The endogenous nature of reserves is obvious in countries that have eliminated reserve requirements, as is the case in Canada, but also in the United Kingdom, Australia and New Zealand, to name a few. Here, the central bank acts as a clearing house and ensures that deficit banks exactly compensate surplus banks. In this case, any overnight rate can ensure clearing. It is then quite clear that the interbank rate, targeted and announced by the central bank, will dominate and act as a benchmark in all negotiations between the banks.

What about open economies?

Up to now, we have ignored a very important component of the central bank's assets: its stock of foreign currencies. In the traditional mainstream open-economy model, the so-called Mundell-Fleming model with fixed exchange rates, any balance of payment surplus would generate an injection of high-powered money resulting from the inflow of foreign currency into commercial bank accounts. This occurs because banks exchange their foreign currency holdings for domestic currency supplied by the central bank. Subsequently, so the story goes, the increase in bank reserves would allow banks to increase lending, which would also increase the supply of money through the standard money multiplier process. The inevitable conclusion, according to neoclassical economists, is that money is endogenous in an open economy with fixed exchange rates.

Is this consistent with the post-Keynesian endogenous version of the story? It is not. One important difference is that in the neoclassical model, the increase in the supply of money is not generated by a prior demand for credit from economic agents: in fact, this increase is completely independent from it.

Therefore it comes as no surprise that post-Keynesians reject this analysis. In its stead, they offer an alternative explanation of what is at work: this is the compensation principle (Lavoie, 2001).

In a monetary production economy, banks are always willing to extend credit to all those who demand it, as long as they are deemed creditworthy. Banks are never required to have excess reserves before doing so. As for foreign currencies, these will be used, in an overdraft system, to reimburse banks' existing debt toward the central bank. With respect to the balance sheet of the central bank, the increase in foreign currency, which in effect is a loan to agents abroad, will be exactly compensated by the decrease in advances to the private banks (loans to the domestic economy). As a result, there will be no change in reserves or the money stock.

A similar mechanism exists in asset-based economies, although in this case, the central bank will initiate the compensation effect, which we can also call an endogenous 'sterilization' effect. To be clear, however, this sterilization is automatic: central banks will willingly absorb the excess reserves while banks are more than happy to get rid of them. In exchange for the reserves, the central bank can offer Treasury bills or repos to the banks, which the latter prefer since they carry a higher return. The central bank can also decide to reduce government deposits held by banks. Either way, all reserves will be absorbed by the end of the day (Godley and Lavoie, 2005–06).

A central bank reaction function

The main conclusion from this analysis is that the central bank can control neither the supply of money nor the supply of high-powered money. In fact, the central bank must always supply the necessary amount of high-powered money required by the banking system. In Canada, for instance, the central bank possesses the ability to calculate rather precisely the exact amount of clearing balances (called settlement balances) required by the banking system as a whole to compensate for the inflows or outflows. For this reason, the Bank of Canada is able to hit its target benchmark rate with extreme precision. In the USA, the situation is a bit different. Because of some minor differences in the the way it operates, the Federal Reserve must rely on an estimate, rather than the exact number, of the amount of reserves required by the banking system. As a result, the federal funds rate will only gravitate around the target rate – the benchmark rate. But this in no way alters the fact that the short-term interest rate may be viewed as an exogenous variable.

The benchmark rate is an administered rate of interest. It is set by the central bank for a given period of time, say a month, or until the central bank decides to change its monetary (interest rate) policy. Hence, while monetary policy remains unchanged, the rate is exogenous for that period of time, irrespective of disturbances in the economy, or the stock of money in existence. Graphically, we can represent this approach by drawing the money supply curve as a horizontal line at the existing benchmark rate.

As just stated, the central bank will change its benchmark in accordance with its specific economic objectives. For instance, the central bank will usually raise the benchmark rate whenever the economy is booming, that is, whenever capacity utilization is high and on the rise or unemployment is low and falling. It will also increase rates whenever inflation is rising relative to the target rate of inflation (or whenever there are expectations that inflation is on the rise). In otherwise tranquil situations, the central bank may also decide to increase the benchmark rate when housing prices or stock market prices are overly high and rising. The benchmark may also be tied to foreign benchmark rates. The central bank benchmark rate may fall whenever the opposite situations occur.

These actions describe what we call the central bank reaction function, the best-known example of which is the so-called Taylor Rule. It should be noted that the rate of interest can no longer be seen as a truly exogenous rate since it depends on other variables of the system. The supply of money must now be described as a series of horizontal curves shifting through time, thereby possibly reinstating a dotted upward-sloping money supply curve, as shown in Figure 3.2, with the H^S curve.

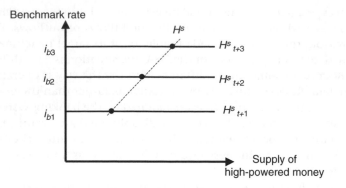

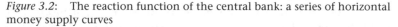

Figure 3.2:   The reaction function of the central bank: a series of horizontal money supply curves

This analysis notwithstanding, post-Keynesians still argue that the benchmark rate is an exogenous rate: the money supply curve is still seen as horizontal at each time period. Whereas it is true that the central bank may want to change the benchmark rate based on events ocurring in the economy, both domestically and abroad, this does not mean that the rate of interest is an endogenous variable. Far from it, since the decision remains very much at the discretion of the central bank. The benchmark interest rate is not a market phenomenon. The central bank can always decline to raise the benchmark, and as a result all short-term interest rates, when economic activity is on the rise.

3.3   The relationship between banks and firms

Initial and final finance

Banks and firms interact in many ways. For instance, firms hold banking deposits and a number of financial assets. Yet, the most important relationship between banks and firms is the debt relationship that exists whenever a bank agrees to grant bank credit (a loan) to fund the production activities of non-financial firms.

The key argument here is time: with the exception of some services, the production of goods and services takes time, and firms must in some way be able to remunerate their employees and pay their suppliers in advance of sales receipts. We could assume of course that firms have some savings from which they can meet their monetary obligations. But in most cases, firms will have to rely on bank loans before production even begins. This *initial* finance is required irrespective of what is being produced. Indeed all firms, whether they produce consumption goods in advance of demand or whether they produce investment goods to order, must rely on loans. Furthermore, this logic applies equally to growing and stationary economies, since banks must always agree to renew a firm's access to finance. In other words, the banks must agree to roll-over debt.

Post-Keynesian economists, along with some proponents of the monetary circuit, such as Graziani (2003), make an important distinction between the initial finance of production, which, as just described, arises whenever a firm borrows funds from the bank, and the *final* finance of investment, which usually takes place on financial markets. Davidson (1982) refers to 'construction finance' and 'investment funding' respectively to distinguish between these two different steps of the financing process.

Firms that purchase capital goods must also be able to finance them. Besides their own finance – their retained earnings – firms must capture the saving of households, either directly or indirectly through the banking system or other financial institutions such as mutual funds or insurance companies. This final finance phase of the production process closes the circuit of production.

Lines of credit

Lines of credit, which are a contract between a bank and a borrower, play an important role in the initial financing of production, since they provide a flexible access to finance. By agreeing to a credit line, firms enter into a contractual agreement with the bank that specifies the maximum amount that can be borrowed when needed, the conditions under which access to the line is given, as well as the rate of interest on the amount being drawn down (Wolfson, 1996). The rate may be fixed, in which case the borrower pays some fee to guarantee the fixed rate; or the rate may vary, in which case its level will be set as a mark-up over some market rate, say the Treasury bill rate. This mark-up is a risk premium imposed by banks to cover default risks as well as administrative costs. As a result, the interest rate on credit lines tends to follow the general evolution of market rates.

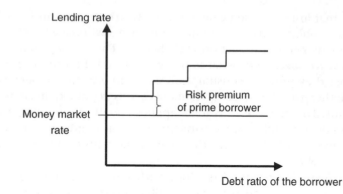

Figure 3.3:   Kalecki's principle of increasing risk

Figure 3.3 shows the rate of interest that would be imposed on firms with different debt loads. With otherwise identical firms, banks will necessarily impose a higher interest rate on those firms burdened by a heavier debt load, due to the perceived higher risk. The same kind of rating will occur when firms issue commercial paper on the financial markets. Figure 3.3 illustrates Kalecki's principle of increasing risk (Kalecki, 1971, ch. 9), first outlined in 1937.

Credit rationing

The endogeneity of money is a central component of post-Keynesian economics. It applies to many dimensions of a monetary economy. First, as discussed above, bank reserves and currency are supplied endogenously by the central bank in response to prior demand. Second, whenever households wish to hold part of their wealth in the form of bank deposits, the latter are also created at households' request. Yet, what can we say about money that agents, households or firms, wish to hold only temporarily, intending to spend it in the near future. In other words, what can we say about credit money? Is bank credit not also endogenous?

On the one hand, post-Keynesians claim that the supply of credit is endogenous, implying that banks always agree to meet the demand from firms passively, while on the other hand they claim that there will always be a 'fringe of unsatisfied customers', to use Keynes's (1930, vol. 2, p. 364) well-known expression. In other words, post-Keynesians recognize that there will be some credit rationing. Are these two arguments consistent? And do they question the endogenous nature of credit money?

In fact, the answer is simple: banks always agree to meet the demand arising from those who are deemed to be creditworthy. Borrowers that do not meet the banks' criteria simply do not receive credit. As long as borrowers are credible – that is, perceived as being able to reimburse their debt – banks will agree to lend to them. Hence, the loans that banks grant are only limited by the availability of good or creditworthy borrowers.

Of course, the obvious question is whether banks can tell who is creditworthy and who is not and banks have developed a number of sophisticated ways of doing this. For instance, borrowers can be assigned to various risk categories, determination of which will be based on the borrowers' history, their past relationship with the bank, the kind of project to be financed, and a number of debt and liquidity ratios, among which will be the borrowers' cash flow relative to the estimated interest burden. Those borrowers who do not meet the required criteria or who decline to fulfil the collateral requirements will be turned down. Of course, individuals or firms meeting all conditions will be given access to a line of credit that will cover their normal financial needs, thereby allowing the production process to begin.

The liquidity preference of banks

The notion of liquidity preference is a central theme of post-Keynesian economics, yet many post-Keynesian believe that it must be understood more broadly (Dow and Dow, 1989). Indeed, while the concept is usually associated with household portfolio decisions regarding choices between holding money and other financial assets, it can nevertheless be extended to include the behaviour of firms and of banks.

In the case of firms, their liquidity preference decisions revolve around whether to purchase financial assets or physical (capital) goods. As for banks, liquidity preference involves their desire to extend bank loans. For instance, banks with high liquidity preference are reluctant to increase loans or to take on new customers. Hence, we can use the concept of liquidity preference in the banking industry to measure the willingness of banks to extend

Box 3.1: A post-Keynesian view of credit rationing

We can distinguish two types of demand for credit. The total demand for credit, which includes the demand from those who are creditworthy and those who are not, can be labelled the 'notional demand' for credit. Yet, since banks only consider those who meet their creditworthiness criteria, for all purposes the only relevant demand is the 'effective demand' for credit, which includes only the borrowers that are creditworthy (Lavoie, 1992a, p. 177; Wolfson, 1996, 2003). If we assume an average lending rate, i_1, credit rationing is depicted by the distance AB. If the rate increases, say to i_2, then fewer firms and fewer households will want to borrow, given the higher costs of borrowing. This is reflected by the negatively-sloped notional demand curve in Figure 3.4. Yet, at the same time, a greater number of borrowers will not meet the borrowing criteria of the banks. In other words, fewer borrowers will be creditworthy. As a result, a greater number of borrowers will be turned down. As interest rates increase, a widening gap arises between the notional and the effective demand curves, as depicted in Figure 3.4.

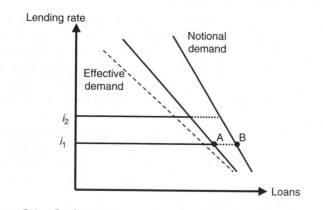

Figure 3.4: Credit rationing: notional and effective demand

Box 3.1: A post-Keynesian view of credit rationing – *cont'd*

As to the rate of interest on loans, we can divide it into two components. There will be a component i_b reflecting the benchmark rate of the central bank and hence the prevailing money market rates (such as the Treasury bill rate or the overnight rate), while the second component will reflect the risk premium, σ. Hence we can write the following:

$$i_l = i_b + \sigma$$

We thus see that see that increases in interest rates on loans can arise from two potential sources. First, since lending rates are essentially based on the benchmark interest rate set by the central bank, any increase in the benchmark rate will lead to an increase in lending rates. Moreover, banks may decide to increase the spread between the lending and the benchmark rate, by increasing the risk premium, σ. The effective demand for loans is drawn for a given risk premium. Hence, when banks decide to increase the risk premium, they are in effect strengthening the criteria needed to get a loan. This translates into a leftward shift of the effective demand curve, as depicted by the shift towards the dotted curve in Figure 3.4. Hence, for every risk premium there exists a specific effective demand curve.

---

credit to potential borrowers. It represents the confidence that banks have over the uncertain future.

Of course, if this is the case, how then can we measure the liquidity of banks? This is certainly not an easy question to answer. Nevertheless, there are a few ways of approaching this issue. For instance, in asset-based systems, where banks hold government securities, we can measure liquidity by considering the risk-free securities to loans ratio. In overdraft economies, we could calculate the bank capital to loans ratio. In fact, this is precisely how the Bank for International Settlements (BIS) calculates the solvency of banks, with the help of the so-called capital adequacy ratios.

There are other ways of measuring the liquidity preference of banks. For instance, when banks become more pessimistic about the future – that is, about the future ability of firms to repay their debt – they will tend to raise their lending criteria. As a result, some firms will no longer qualify to receive a bank loan. Banks will require firms to have lower debt loads, better cash flows, or higher collateral requirements.

Hence, we can say that in times of uncertainty, liquidity preference increases, carrying with it two important consequences. First, lending rates will be higher. Indeed, since banks expect more defaults on loans, they will want to protect their own rate of return by increasing the risk premium to compensate for the increased risk. Second, given the more stringent criteria, a number of borrowers will now be denied a loan: they simply are no longer considered creditworthy.

Note, moreover, that this same kind of behaviour rules financial markets. When markets are worried, the spread between yields on government securities and junk bonds increases, which serves as a good leading indicator of the state of the economy.

Financial fragility and the paradox of tranquillity

While banks may use a variety of approaches to assess the creditworthiness of borrowers, it remains nonetheless true that these decisions are highly subjective. They are a matter of confidence. Hyman Minsky (1976, 1981) is a post-Keynesian whose pioneering work about the behaviour of banks and their borrowers has helped to show the instability that may result from such interactions.

Minsky, whose work has become highly popular among both post-Keynesian and radical economists, has developed a Wall Street view of the economy known as either the financial instability hypothesis (FIH) or the financial fragility hypothesis (FFH). In contrast to some other finance specialists, such as Gordon (1997), who believe that more wealthy entrepreneurs will become more prudent, Minsky asserts that households, firms and banks are willing to adopt more risky behaviour and strategies in periods of economic boom or after a long period of high growth. Minsky argues that in such situations banks ease their risk premia as well as their lending criteria, accepting higher debt loads (higher ρ parameters, as represented in Chapter 2). In addition, all agents – that is households, firms and banks – will willingly hold smaller proportions of less liquid assets. This is the paradox of tranquillity: stability breeds instability.

A period of relative stability and high economic activity will eventually lead to more fragile financial conditions. More speculative behaviour will also accompany greater financial fragility. Indeed, firms and banks will compete against one another using debt as a lever; households will soon follow suit, thereby generating rising stock market prices and rising real estate values. Eventually, the central bank will weigh in and impose credit constraints or – as is probably more the case today – it will raise the benchmark rate.

Given the higher debt loads, higher rates of interest will further erode the fragility of the system making it more difficult to meet the interest payments on existing debt. At this point, banks will surely change their behaviour by tightening both their risk premia and their lending criteria. All this may translate into a stock market crash, unless governments stand ready to support aggregate demand and the economy by engaging in large deficit spending (see the numerous papers in Bellofiore and Ferri, 2001).

Minsky's financial fragility hypothesis serves to show quite well how a cyclical series of virtuous and vicious circles may have nothing to do with the real economy. In fact, Minsky ties economic fluctuations to unstable financial conventions and the greedy behaviour of all economic agents. He also emphasizes the insufficient power of regulatory bodies to monitor this behaviour.

3.4 A systemic view of the monetary economy

While the discussion above has served us well, it is time to consider money and the monetary circuit from a more systematic point of view. The French circuit writers have always advocated a mesoeconomic approach, that is the study of structural – or macroeconomic – laws, independent of the behaviour of agents.

Mesoeconomics is found halfway between the macroeconomic emphasis on effective demand and the microeconomic analysis of agents. With respect to technical conditions and relative prices, Leontief's and Sraffa's input–output models are an integral component of mesoeconomic analysis.

To enable a better understanding of the monetary circuit, mesoeconomic analysis rests on monetary relations, more specifically on the interactions of sector-based balance sheets and financial flows.

The principles of a systemic monetary analysis

In the last few years, a number of post-Keynesians have adopted the use of matrices better to explore mesoeconomic relations. Inspired largely by the work of Wynne Godley (1999) and Lance Taylor (2004), but also by that of Eichner (1987), I believe that such an approach constitutes an important new way of uniting heterodox macroeconomists, helping to replace and dismiss the neoclassical concept of constrained maximization. This new approach also shares many points of interest with the macroeconomic work of James Tobin (1982), himself a neoclassical synthesis Keynesian. In fact, in his Bank of Sweden Nobel Prize acceptance speech, Tobin explained why his approach is different from that of the standard neoclassical model. According to Tobin, a proper macroeconomics must entertain four important characteristics:

- Stocks and flows must be fully integrated into the analysis, and their accounting must be done in a fully coherent manner.
- All models should include a multitude of sectors and of assets, each with its own rate of return.
- It is important to incorporate all monetary and financial operations, and thus integrate the central bank and commercial banks.
- There cannot be any 'black holes'. All flows must inevitably have an origin and a destination. All budget and portfolio adding-up constraints must be respected. This holds both for behavioural relations and for the actual values of the variables.

Tobin was working at Yale University, in New Haven, Connecticut, and this approach is often referred to as the New Haven school. At the same time, in the 1970s, a closely related methodology and approach were independently developed and advocated by Godley and his colleagues in the Department of Applied Economics at the University of Cambridge, leading to the creation of the so-called 'new Cambridge' model (Godley and Cripps, 1983).

While neoclassical economists have rejected Tobin's approach and have fallen back on the unrealistic 'representative agent', where consumers and producers are one and the same, some post-Keynesians have embraced Tobin's approach, incorporating it into a monetary production economy where the supply of money is endogenous and where behavioural equations respond to Kaleckian or Keynesian precepts rather than neoclassical ones.

What Godley's and Tobin's analyses emphasize is the need for a coherent macroeconomic framework that links the flow dimension of macroeconomics with the stock dimension of real capital, financial assets and debts and their corresponding rates of return.

Sectoral balance sheets and financial flows

Tobin's and Godley's systemic approach rests on two matrices: a balance-sheet matrix and a transactions-flow matrix. Balance sheets deal with stocks, both tangible and financial ones. Tangible stocks include machines and buildings (the fixed capital of firms), as well as the value of real estate held by households. Tangible stocks also include durable goods such as cars still in circulation. We may also wish to include the inventory stocks of firms (S) – goods which are produced but have yet to be sold. These tangible stocks have no counterpart in the balance sheet.

Financial assets, on the other hand, do have a counterpart, which is debt and which appears on the asset side of another agent's or sector's balance sheet (household, producing firms, banks, the government or the central bank). For instance, loans made by banks are an asset for the bank, but a liability for the borrower.

Where do these stocks come from? The answer is that they are either the result of flows, which are added to the existing stocks; or they result from the re-evaluation of certain assets, an exercise that is excluded from the transactions-flow matrix.

Each stock is then associated with a given flow through a dynamic equation, which links the past and the present. For instance, the value of all shares held by households at the end of a given year, E, is equal by definition to the stock of shares held at a given time, e, and the price of the shares, p_e. This value can be said to arise from three distinct sources: the value of the shares held at the end of the previous year (that is at the beginning of the current year); the value of the new shares issued by firms and purchased by households at market prices during the current year; and the capital gain resulting from the increase in the price of the shares that were held at the beginning of the year over the course of that same year.

The integration of national account flows with financial flows

The transactions-flow matrix is an interesting tool because it can link all the important aggregates of the National Income and Product Accounts (NIPA) to the financial flows that impact balance sheets. The matrix describes a vertically-integrated production economy, dealing with value-added only, as in NIPA, abstracting from the maze of interdependencies associated with intermediate production.

Table 3.2 presents the essential elements of this approach, although we excluded, for purposes of simplification only, the central bank as well as the state. In that sense, it is a pure Wicksellian model.

To simplify further, we also assume that banks do not make profits (we set the rate of interest on loans, i_l, equal to the rate of interest on money deposits, i_m), that households do not borrow from banks, and that firms do not hold money balances.

One of the advantages of using accounting matrices is that they guarantee that nothing gets lost in the discussion: as stated above, all flows must come from somewhere and must end up somewhere. This explains why each line and column add to zero: the matrix is perfectly balanced.

Horizontally, each flow has an equivalent counterpart. Overall, the rows describe the nominal amounts that are being exchanged from one sector to another. The equality between the inflow and the outflow arises for one of the following three reasons. First, supply may always adjust itself to demand, either because production adjusts or through changes in inventory stocks; second, demand may be rationed (as in the case of credit rationing); third, market prices may provide for an instantaneous adjustment between supply and demand (as in financial markets). This explains why it is easier to work within a closed economy; otherwise, in an open economy, the matrix would obviously have to consider the rest of the world.

Vertically, each transaction must be financed. The columns sum to zero and represent the budget constraints that each of the sectors must respect. Let us begin by considering households, which face an obvious budget constraint: they receive interest payments ($+ i_m D_{(-1)}$), dividends (F_D) and wages (wN), with which they can consume (C), increase their bank deposits (ΔD), or purchase newly-issued shares on the financial market ($p_e \Delta e$).

Table 3.2: The transactions-flow matrix in a closed economy without government

Account	Households	Firms Current	Firms Capital	Banks Current	Banks Capital	Σ
Consumption	$-C$	$+C$				0
Investment		$+I$	$-I$			0
inventory stocks		$+\Delta S$	$-\Delta S$			0
Wages	$+wN$	$-wN$				0
Net profits	$+F_D$	$-(P_{ND}+P_D)$	$+P_{ND}$			0
Interest on loans		$-i_l L_{(-1)}$		$+i_l L_{(-1)}$		0
Interest on deposits	$+i_m D_{(-1)}$			$-i_m D_{(-1)}$		0
in loans			$+\Delta L_f$		$-\Delta L_b$	0
in deposits	$-\Delta D_m$				$+\Delta D_b$	0
Shares on financial markets	$-p_e\,\Delta e$		$+p_e\,\Delta e$			0
Σ	0	0	0	0	0	0

With respect to firms, their situation is slightly more complicated. While they sell consumption goods (C) to households, they also sell investment goods (I) to each other, as well as finished goods not yet sold to customers, ΔS.

The income generated from these sales, either realized or based on an accounting entry, must always equal the wage and interest payments, plus the net profits from the private sector. These profits can be further divided into two components: dividends P_D to households, and retained earnings, P_{ND}, which are a component of the final financing of fixed capital and inventory stocks.

The sources and uses of funds

In the flow matrix, all components with a positive sign represent a source of funds. For instance, wages, given by wN, which is the product of nominal wages, w, and employment, N, is a source of funds for households. Yet, they also represent a use of funds from the point of view of the production sector, and so carry a negative sign when entered in the column of the firms.

The bottom of the matrix represents changes in claims and liabilities. Inasmuch as households increase either their holdings of equities (a quantity of shares e times the price of the shares p_e) or of bank deposits, ΔD, this implies a use of funds and therefore a negative sign. But when a firm gets a new bank loan, ΔL, which increases its stock of debt, it becomes a source of funds for the production sector, meaning that it should carry a positive sign.

Readers should note that the terminology 'source and use of funds' may lead to some confusion when discussing the role of banks. When a bank lends and, in doing so, increases the stock of outstanding loans, the additional loans are assigned a negative sign in the transactions-flow matrix. The corresponding deposits that are being created as a result carry a positive sign. In this sense, we can claim that from the point of view of the banking sector, deposits are a 'source' of funds whereas loans are the 'use' of funds. A note of caution is here required: this *may* give the impression that deposits are therefore required to make a loan, but this would be a misleading inference. Rather, as post-Keynesians argue, loans make deposits. In other words, while the increase in deposits may be seen as a source of funds from a financial perspective, the causal element remains nevertheless the loans initially granted by banks. These loans are created *ex nihilo* at the request of firms who are considered creditworthy by banks (Lavoie, 2003).

The creation of money

We have now established the main elements of post-Keynesian monetary theory. In section 3.3, for instance, we discussed the crucial distinction between initial and final finance. In this context, therefore, how can we explain the monetary circuit? We can answer this question by referring to the transactions-flow matrix developed above and illustrated in Table 3.2; in doing so, we can provide a better explanation of the crucial difference between initial and final finance.

The production sector of the transactions-flow matrix is further subdivided into a capital account and a current account. Both accounts must sum to zero. The capital account column describes the components of final finance. In this simple model, the accumulation of fixed capital or the increase in inventories of firms at the end of the period, say a quarter or even a year, is financed by only three possible sources: new share issues, new borrowing from banks, or undistributed profits (retained earnings).

By contrast, the shaded cells in the matrix represent initial finance. At the beginning of the production process, as the monetary circuit begins, firms must borrow the funds needed to pay wages to employees, and begin the production of new goods, ΔS (recall that we assume a closed vertically integrated production economy, where the only costs are wage costs). The amount borrowed is exactly equal to total wages in the current period. It is the first stage of the circuit. It does not matter whether loans are taken for the production of consumption or investment goods: both in fact require initial finance.

At the very beginning of the circuit, therefore, firms have a debt towards banks but also a claim in the form of a bank deposit. This first stage is in fact very short: firms will draw on their line of credit only when they need to pay wages and begin production. This is done either through cheques or through electronic transfers, as is usually the case nowadays. But as soon as wages are paid, they become an income for households and workers. At the very moment they are paid, and hence before households begin consuming the newly received income, these funds simultaneously become household savings, ΔD_m. The shaded cells depict this second stage.

The third stage – final finance – as already pointed out, is represented by the capital account of the production sector, when firms collect back funds from households.

Accounting principles and quadruple accounting

Using matrices allows us in fact to fall back on some useful accounting principles, especially when considering the operations of firms. As goods are produced but remain unsold, they become an additional component of inventory stocks, ΔS. Consistent with the best accounting practices, it is important that inventory goods be valued at their current production costs or at least at their replacement cost (and not at their expected sale price).

In our vertically integrated economy, the cost of production of these stocks is exactly equal to the wages paid to households within this period. In this sense, the value of the increase in inventories, ΔS, is exactly equal to wN, which is what is emphasized by the shaded cells in the current account column of the firms.

The use of flow matrices also makes the 'quadruple accounting' principle more evident (Copeland, 1949). This is because since each column and each row must sum to zero at all times, any transaction requires at least four recorded changes for the matrix to balance out. For instance, if a bank decides to grant a loan ΔL to the production sector, it must also create, as a counterpart, deposits ΔD of an equal amount. The capital account column of the banking sector then sums to zero. Moreover, the new loan must also be recorded as an additional liability in the capital account of the producing sector. This ensures that the row of loans sums to 0. But a fourth entry must be changed to take into account the fact that the producing sector now holds an additional amount of bank deposits, which allows the row of deposits to sum to zero as well. As a result, we have a minimum of four accounting records for each transaction.

Models and the role of the flow matrices

Alongside sector-based balance-sheet matrices, sectoral transactions-flow matrices provide the core relationships of monetary production economies. To these, along with the dynamic equations that link stocks and flows, we should add behavioural equations pertaining to each sector of the economy.

Any model offers specific behavioural equations that provide the closure of the model and account for its particular results and derived conclusions. Nevertheless, post-Keynesians like Godley believe that the core accounting equations and the dynamic stock-flow equations actually constitute a framework that constrains the range of possible results. In other words, certain configurations or dynamics are just plain impossible, because they would contradict the accounting core. As pointed out by Taylor (2004, p. 2), stock-flow consistent macro modelling and the core accounting equations 'remove many degrees of freedom from possible configurations of patterns of payments at the macro level'.

According to Godley, any fully-coherent model that adequately represents a monetary economy of production will necessarily give some medium and long-term results that are essentially identical, irrespective of the values given to the various parameters. Such a model must be able to provide a linkage between all stocks and flows, while taking all transaction flows into account, including the budget constraints. In addition, stock constraints, such as portfolio constraints and asset adding-up constraints, must be accounted for.

Economic agents target certain ratios that will guarantee the confluence of both stocks and flows, for instance, desired sales to inventory stocks ratio in the case of firms. In fact, this may arise without the express knowledge of agents. For example, when households consume each year a given ratio of their income and wealth, they implicitly define a long-term steady relationship between wealth (a stock) and disposable income (a flow).

What can we learn from a systemic approach?

Post-Keynesian models that follow the principles presented in this section allow us to verify the main characteristics developed earlier in section 3.1. While the supply of and the demand for money are subject to different and independent constraints (the supply of money is constrained by the balance sheets of central banks and commercial banks; whereas the demand for money is constrained by households' portfolio choices), they are necessarily equal in any fully coherent model, even if there are no specific equations that explicitly force their equality.

This should help us understand the irrelevance of the neoclassical argument suggesting that excess money is the underlying cause of inflation. For post-Keynesians, inflation can never be caused by an excess supply of money.

We can also show how the central bank and the Treasury can directly set interest rates. Yet, whereas central banks can always control the short-term interest rate, they can also control the long-term interest rate if they so desire. If this were the case, the central bank would have to accept large variations in the composition of its liabilities, that is the proportion of short-term and long-term securities. Otherwise, the long-term rate would fluctuate wildly relative to the short-term rate, even if arbitrage forces would slowly but eventually ensure that long-term rates approximate the expected future short-term rates. These expected rates are to a large extent determined by recently observed short-term rates that themselves converge towards the benchmark rate, as long as the central bank is willing to enforce it with sufficient determination and persistence.

Systemic analysis also shows us how, in an open economy, external disequilibria in no way undermine the ability of the central bank to set the benchmark interest rate of its choice. The only true constraint, in a fixed exchange rate regime, is that external disequilibria do not automatically resolve themselves, so much so that the eventual lack of exchange reserves will force the state to pursue restrictive fiscal and monetary policies.

As we will see in Chapter 5, there thus exists a deflationary bias in an open economy framework. Countries with an external surplus are never constrained into pursuing the expansionary policies that would compensate for the restrictive economic policies put in place by countries with external deficits.

4
The Short Period: Effective Demand and the Labour Market

The main objective of this chapter is to examine the role of effective demand and its impact on the labour market. As stated in Chapter 1, the claim that economies are demand-led is a crucial argument of post-Keynesian economics. In fact, effective demand is a key factor of the theory of employment. Contrary to neoclassical theory, as we shall see, a decrease in real wages does not increase the demand for labour. Rather, the opposite is true: an increase in real wages leads to an increase in consumption, which in turn increases the demand for labour and decreases unemployment. As a result, an increase in the minimum wage and in the average wage will have beneficial effects on employment and the overall economy – a conclusion that stands in contrast to what is assumed by those who defend TINA.

The analysis in this chapter will limit itself to the short period. Any and all elements of long-period analysis are left to the next chapter.

Short and long periods

Before proceeding any further, it is important to clarify the difference between short and long-period analysis. There are in fact two possible interpretations.

The first distinction is the one we often find in neoclassical textbooks. There the long period is defined as a state of fully realized expectations, most often those related to prices and inflation. The short period is associated, therefore, with either frustrated price expectations or expectations that have not been fully adjusted.

The second distinction between short and long periods is more formally a distinction between actual periods of time. Indeed, the short period treats the stock of capital goods as given, whereas the long period allows investment flows to alter the existing capital stock. The long period therefore depicts either a stationary economy, where households' real wealth is constant and where net investment (net of capital depreciation) is nil, or a growing economy where capital stock and household wealth are growing exponentially.

A short-period analysis based on this second definition is necessarily limited. Indeed, as we discussed in the previous chapter, a fully coherent analysis must link all stocks and flows. By postulating that the stocks of capital and household wealth are constant, even though firms invest and households save, we omit some of the most important consequences of their decisions. As such, any discussion under these terms can only be a snapshot of the economy in which periods are linked to one another in time. A good example of this mistreatment of time, as Tobin (1979, ch. 4) reminds us, is the IS-LM model of the neoclassical synthesis, which determines positive saving and investment without ever taking into consideration their impact on wealth and productive capacity.

Short-period analysis as defined in this chapter will ignore the effects of investment on the capital stock (the second definition). We will, however, assume that expectations are realized by assuming that the goods market is in equilibrium, supply having had time to adapt itself to the demand for goods (in contrast to the first definition).

4.1 Effective demand and its components

Autonomous and induced expenditures

In standard neoclassical models, aggregate demand depends essentially on two components: fiscal policy and the supply of money. Yet, since the supply of money is an endogenous variable in post-Keynesian models, it cannot be a causal element in determining effective demand. As for fiscal policy, we will put it aside by adopting a simplified model: we will assume a closed economy with no government. In such a simplified model, what then are the determinants of aggregate demand?

In the *General Theory*, Keynes (1936, ch. 3) distinguishes between autonomous and induced expenditures as components of effective demand. By induced expenditures, we mean the components of current aggregate demand that are dependent upon the current level of income. In contrast, autonomous expenditures are independent of current output. In a closed economy with no government, the only remaining components of aggregate demand are consumption and investment.

For Keynes, investment is basically an independent variable which depends on the long-run expectations of entrepreneurs. Consumption, however, is partially induced. In fact, this approach is largely consistent with that of Kalecki (1971, ch. 8), who considers investment to be independent of current output, and who divides consumption into two components: consumption out of wages (workers) and consumption out of profits (capitalists). Whereas the former is induced, the second is an autonomous variable since it depends on lagged realized profits.

A macroeconomic determination of profits

In Kalecki (1971, ch. 7), the equations explaining macroeconomic profits are fairly simple. Anchoring his analysis in national accounting, Kalecki's equations are consistent with the transactions-flow matrix developed in the previous chapter, specifically the current account column of producing firms. We may approach the national product from two different angles: an incomes approach or an expenditure approach. Nominal income Y is defined as follows:

$$Y = Wages + Profits = Consumption + Investment$$

Given the subdivision of consumption discussed above, we may write the following:

$$Wages + Profits = Consumption\ out\ of\ wages$$
$$+ Consumption\ out\ of\ profits + Investment$$

We can further assume, as do Kalecki and most classical authors before him, especially Marx, that workers spend all their income, that is they have no saving. Hence, we can write:

$$Consumption\ out\ of\ wages = Wages$$

Plugging this into the previous equation yields Kalecki's famous profit equation, which he first outlined in Polish in 1933:

Profits = Consumption out of profits + Investment

One of the main conclusions we can draw from this insight is that in a closed economy without government, where workers do not save, macroeconomic profits are exactly equal to the investment of the private sector plus capitalists' consumption out of profits.

The causality in Kalecki's equation

But what is the exact meaning of this equation, and what can we say about the causality implied by the equation? How can we interpret its conclusions? This is a question that Kalecki asked, and to which he provided the following answer:

> What is the significance of this equation? Does it mean that profits in a given period determine capitalists' consumption and investment, or the reverse of this? The answer to this question depends on which of these items is directly subject to the decisions of capitalists. Now it is clear that capitalists can decide to consume and to invest more in a given period than in the preceding one, but they cannot decide to earn more. It is, therefore, their investment and consumption decisions which determine profits, and not vice versa.
>
> (Kalecki, 1971, pp. 78–9)

We can summarize this macroeconomic theory by referring to an aphorism made famous by Kaldor (1956, p. 96), although often wrongly attributed to Kalecki: 'Capitalists earn what they spend, and workers spend what they earn.' This statement highlights an important asymmetry: capitalists and entrepreneurs can always decide to spend more (provided banks accept to finance them), whereas workers cannot decide to earn more, since this depends essentially on the employment they are being offered by entrepreneurs.

4.2 The Kaleckian model

Keynes or Kalecki?

In *The General Theory of Employment, Interest and Money*, largely inspired by the work of his teacher Alfred Marshall, Keynes (1936)

Box 4.1: A rejection of the crowding-out effect

Those who defend the virtues of TINA often argue that expansionary fiscal policies designed to support aggregate demand are doomed to fail. They argue that, with deficit spending, governments use resources that could be put to better use by the private sector for investment purposes. This is the so-called crowding-out effect, also called the 'Treasury view' when Keynes was objecting to it in the 1930s. According to the Treasury view, increases in government deficits crowd out private investment and lead to rising interest rates.

Post-Keynesians reject this approach altogether, and this for several reasons. First, as stated in the previous chapter, market interest rates essentially depend on the benchmark interest rate set by the central bank. Second, we can easily show, using a generalized version of Kalecki's equation, that fiscal deficits actually enhance the profits of the private sector. In fact, it could be argued that there is a reversed crowding-out effect, sometimes called a crowding-in effect. We can show this by rewriting Kalecki's equation and including the government sector. Following Kalecki (1971, p. 82), we get:

Profits net of taxes = Consumption out of profits + Investment + Budget deficits

---

accepts without hesitation some fundamental postulates of neoclassical theory. For instance, he assumes that the stock of money is a given, and he accepts the assumption that firms maximize their profits under the constraint of diminishing returns, hypotheses that we specifically rejected in chapters 2 and 3.

Keynes kept these neoclassical features because he wanted to show his contemporaries that his was a more *general* theory. In his effort to get a fair hearing and to get his message across, Keynes endeavoured to make sure that his arguments would look familiar and would be understood by his colleagues. Unfortunately, Keynes's strategy carries certain shortcomings, which have repercussions up to this day. For instance, fundamentalist post-Keynesians, such as Davidson and Weintraub, insist on following Keynes's method.

Box 4.2: A more formalized profit equation

In order to continue our discussion of effective demand, it is perhaps best to develop more formally Kalecki's profit equation. Using notations from the previous chapter, let us consider national accounting identities. Accordingly, we can define the national product as follows:

$$Y = wN + P = C + I$$

where

$$C = pa_c = pa_{cc} + pa_{cw}$$
$$I = pa_i$$

income is the sum of the wage bill, wN, and profits, P, these being inclusive of interest payments. C and I are respectively nominal consumption and investment expenditures, whereas a_c and a_i are consumption and investment in *real* terms; p is price. Finally, a_{cc} and a_{cw} are the real consumption expenditures of capitalists and workers respectively.

Assuming once again that workers do not save, we obtain the following profit equation:

$$P = pa_{cc} + pa_i$$

According to Kalecki, macroeconomic profits are predetermined since they depend on realized investment, the decisions on which were taken in the past. As for capitalists' consumption, it depends on the amount of profits that were also realized in the past (or on capital gains on financial markets).

In real terms, both capitalist investment and consumption in any given period are thus autonomous variables. Given that investment is a controversial topic in economics, taking it as an exogenous variable is perhaps the best strategy within a short-period analysis.

Macroeconomic profits therefore depend on *real* autonomous expenditures, $a = a_{cc} + a_i$. We can thus rewrite the previous equation as:

$$P = pa$$

Whatever firms do with respect to unit labour costs and real wages, overall (real) profits within the period are here entirely determined by overall real autonomous expenditures.

Box 4.3: The aggregate demand equation

At the macroeconomic level, at least in our simplified model of a closed economy with no government, demand depends on only two components: the induced consumption of workers (their wages), and the autonomous expenditures, which include capitalists' consumption and investment. We can thus write aggregate demand in the following way:

$$AD = wN + pa$$

If we divide AD by p, we obtain aggregate demand in real terms:

$$RAD = (w/p)N + a$$

Thus, in contrast to neoclassical theory, where aggregate demand depends on the supply of money, aggregate demand in post-Keynesian models depends on the wage bill and real autonomous expenditures – that is, on the consumption and investment decisions of capitalists.

As a result, their own version of post-Keynesian theory is rooted in aggregate supply analysis with diminishing returns, and thus shows some similarities with the analysis developed by disequilibrium Keynesians, such as Malinvaud and Bénassy, or Barro and Grossman.

Kalecki, however, was schooled in Marx, not Marshall. As such, in his first articles on the business cycles and effective demand, Kalecki finds no room for neoclassical assumptions. In particular, he readily accepts the notion that production can be increased at constant unit costs. The Kaleckian approach to effective demand is often considered a superior or better approach than Keynes's. This was the conclusion reached in particular by Robinson (1973, p. 97) and Kaldor (1983, p. 15). Indeed, to bring out the radical content of Keynesian economics, one must learn 'from Kalecki rather than from Keynes' (Bhaduri, 1986, p. ix). For some heterodox economists, it is therefore best to speak of Kaleckian economics, rather than post-Keynesian economics (Dostaler, 1988, p. 134).

Box 4.4:　An alternative profit equation

Several post-Keynesians have slightly modified Kalecki's profit equation by omitting any reference to time lags. In many of their models, the consumption of capitalists simply depends on the amount of profits realized during the current period. Assuming that capitalists save a portion s_c of their profits, their consumption is equal to:

$$pa_{cc} = (1 - s_c)P$$

By substituting this in the profit equation, we get:

$$P = p(a_i/s_c) = I/s_c$$

This is the so-called Cambridge short-period profit equation found in Kaldor (1956, p. 96), who ties this equation to Kalecki's profit equations and to Keynes's (1930) 'widow's cruse' analogy. Keynes was then making a reference to the Old Testament story in the First Book of Kings (17), whereby a widow was assured that her barrel of meat and jar of oil would never get depleted. Keynes (1930, p. 139) argued that 'however much of their profits entrepreneurs spend on consumption, the increment of wealth belonging to entrepreneurs remains the same as before. Thus profits, as a source of capital increment for entrepreneurs, are a widow's cruse which remains undepleted however much of them may be devoted to riotous living.' As Kaldor points out, the same can be said about the investment of entrepreneurs.

In post-Keynesian economics, macroeconomic profits are proportional to investment expenditures and inversely proportional to the capitalists' propensity to save out of profits. In the next chapter, we will make use of a dynamic version of this relation. For now, however, let us keep Kalecki's version.

The post-Keynesian utilization function

The Kaleckian aggregate supply curve is based on the theory of the modern firm developed in Chapter 2. The Kaleckian model assumes a more modern version of the production function, which post-

Keynesians call a *utilization function* (Nell, 1988, p. 106), and which assumes no decreasing returns, as long as capacity utilization is below 100 per cent. Constant returns prevail. First proposed by Joan Robinson in 1964, the utilization function implies that firms can hire more or less labour with a given capital equipment, which is utilized at different intensity levels.

Regarding labour, Kaleckian models, like Kalecki himself, generally consider two types of labour: variable (blue-collar or direct) labour and fixed (overhead or indirect) labour (Asimakopulos, 1975). Variable labour is directly related to the production of goods and services; hence it is a variable factor of production. Variable labour wages are a component of the direct costs of firms. Fixed or overhead labour, on the other hand, is not related to production, and consists of so-called white-collar employees and other administrative staff.

While this is an important distinction, which in particular allows us to understand certain fluctuations in average wages through the cycle (Lavoie, 1996–97), we will disregard it for the purpose of our analysis. Yet, despite this simplification, we will still be able to show some of the more fundamental conclusions of the Kaleckian model. In particular, we will see how employment is positively related to real wages.

The Kaleckian paradox of costs

The Kaleckian labour demand curve, as shown in Figure 4.1, illustrates that for a given level of real autonomous expenditures, a, there is a positive relationship between the real wage and the overall level of employment. An increase in the real wage w/p translates into a movement along the effective labour demand curve, and hence to a higher level of employment. This is a complete reversal of the neoclassical theory of employment and of the claims made by TINA advocates.

At first glance, this conclusion may appear paradoxical. Yet it clarifies an important fallacy of composition: what may be good for an individual firm is unhealthy for the economy as a whole if all firms act in the same way.

While it is true that each individual firm could increase its profits by lowering its unit wage costs – if it acted alone – overall profits will not in the end be any higher. Once all firms have lowered

---

Box 4.5: The formalization of the Kaleckian model

The Kaleckian labour-market model is fairly simple. We begin with the real aggregate demand function developed earlier:

$$RAD = (w/p)N + a$$

We then replace the neoclassical production function with the post-Keynesian utilization function, which is directly proportional to the quantity of labour used in production. We have the following equation:

$$q = TN$$

where T, a constant, represents output per worker. In other words, it measures workers' productivity ($T = 1/n$; it is the inverse of the technical coefficient n, the amount of work per unit of output, discussed in Chapter 2). It is an aggregate measure of the degree of advancement of technology, which explains why we are using the letter T to explain this productivity.

By equating supply and demand in real terms, that is $q = RAD$, we get either one of the following equations describing the *effective* labour demand curve (also called the employment curve):

$$N^{Deff} = a/[T-(w/p)]$$
$$(w/p)^{eff} = T - a/N$$

Either of these two equations represents the locus of all points where the goods market is in equilibrium, that is, where saving and investment are equal. In other words, for every real wage–employment combination on this effective labour demand curve, all produced goods are sold at the price set by firms, as shown in Figure 4.1 below. The area below the curve represents a situation of aggregate excess supply in the goods market, while the area above the curve depicts a situation where aggregate demand is greater than aggregate supply (investment exceeds saving). As long as firms react to a situation of excess supply (demand) by reducing (increasing) production, the economy will

---

Box 4.5: The formalization of the Kaleckian model – *cont'd*

move towards the locus of equilibria, that is towards the effective labour demand curve. In other words, the model exhibits stability under these conditions. This is precisely what we shall assume for the rest of this chapter. For simplicity therefore, we presume that the economy is always on the effective labour demand curve.

Note, as well, that in our model, the effective labour demand curve has a positive slope, in contrast to the labour demand curve of neoclassical theory. The Kaleckian labour demand curve is asymptotic to the horizontal line representing productivity per worker, at T. As such, the real wage can never exceed the productivity of blue-collar workers, otherwise firms would make losses.

At the macroeconomic level, therefore, modern firms face only one constraint: effective demand. Each firm would prefer producing and selling more since it knows that higher production does not lead to rising unit costs, at least until full capacity is reached. Firms, however, are constrained by their share of the market.

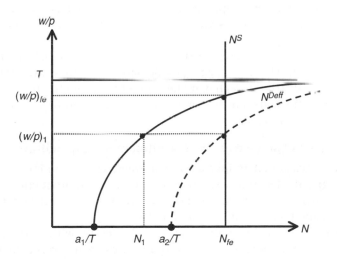

Figure 4.1: The Kaleckian labour market

wages and, by keeping prices constant, increased their mark-ups, they will end up selling fewer goods. As Kalecki (1971, p. 26) reminds us, 'one of the main features of the capitalist system is the fact that what is to the advantage of a single entrepreneur does not necessarily benefit all entrepreneurs as a class'. This is the Kaleckian paradox of costs, which is not dissimilar from the Keynesian paradox of thrift.

According to the paradox of thrift, a well-known concept of principles of macroeconomics, an increase in the marginal propensity to save of households in no way increases aggregate saving and national income. In fact, as long as investment is given and hence autonomous, an increase in the propensity to save cannot have an effect on aggregate saving. The attempt to save more will only translate itself into a reduction in national income, in sales, and in aggregate employment.

Similarly, within the context of the paradox of costs, for any given level of real autonomous expenditures, a decrease in real wages will have no impact on aggregate profits since they only depend on the level of real aggregate expenditures (or on real investment expenditures and the propensity to save out of profits in Kalecki's formula). While the lower real wages are associated with higher profit margins per unit sold (an increase in the θ or Θ costing margin parameter in Chapter 2), national income, sales and employment fall, leaving the overall amount of macroeconomic profits unchanged.

The decrease in aggregate demand is the culprit behind this phenomenon. The fall in aggregate demand arises from the change in income distribution that makes workers worse-off; since their propensity to consume is higher than that of profit recipients, aggregate demand falls.

The impact of an increase in real autonomous expenditures

While it is clear that an increase in real wages leads to an increase in real aggregate demand, and thereby an increase in production and employment, may there not be another way of increasing production and reaching full employment?

Kalecki's – and Keynes's – analysis leaves us with very little choice: the only other solution is to increase autonomous expenditures, *a*. Whenever there is an increase in autonomous expenditures, the effective labour demand curve shifts downwards. Hence, to maintain the same level of real aggregate demand, real wages would need to be lowered. Yet, if real wages stay the same, any increase in autonomous expenditures will generate an increase in employment, as it would in the standard Keynesian model. To show this, consider the dotted curve in Figure 4.1: for a given real wage $(w/p)_1$, an increase in real autonomous expenditures from a_1 to a_2 leads to an increase in employment from N_1 to N_{fe}.

Of course, we need to ask why autonomous expenditures would increase in the first place. Remember that there are two components to autonomous expenditures: consumption out of profits and investment expenditures. Keynes (1936) argues that a decrease in interest rates initiated by the central bank should lead to an increase in these expenditures, although he believes that their effect might be insufficient even when interest rates are brought down to their lowest levels. This is why Keynes relies on public expenditures to decrease persistent unemployment.

Keynes's contemporaries, however, such as Pigou, as well as some neoclassical economists like Don Patinkin, have argued that public expenditures were not necessary to re-establish full employment. They claimed that unemployment will eventually lead to a decrease in nominal wages and prices, provided of course that they are sufficiently flexible. As a result, private autonomous expenditures will increase on their own, because of the greater purchasing power provided by the money balances held by households. According to this neoclassical view, market forces will eventually eliminate unemployment. This argument is known as the real balance effect or the wealth effect.

Post-Keynesians, however, have no faith in the self-adjusting wisdom of markets. First, such a mechanism cannot exist in a world where both money and wealth are endogenous variables, as we saw in Chapter 3. Second, as Keynes (1936, ch. 19) and Tobin (1979, ch. 1) remind us, falling prices can have perverse effects on the firm and on the economy. For instance, they can increase the real burden of debt, thereby triggering bankruptcies and chaos, which would exacerbate the existing stagnation or recession.

Box 4.6: The paradoxes of cost and thrift with the Cambridge equation

In the simple Keynesian textbook model, saving is always in a simple relation, s, to income. As such, consumption can be defined simply as a proportion $(1 - s)$ of income. Given equilibrium conditions in the goods market, the equality between saving and investment suggests the following relationship between output and real investment:

$$q = a_i / s$$

with of course the well-known Keynesian multiplier, $1/s$.

If we consider the Cambridge equation, where workers do not save and capitalists save a proportion s_c out of profits, as was suggested earlier, the equality between saving and investment implies the following equation:

$$q = a_i T / \{s_c(T - w/p)\}$$

This equation allows us quickly to verify the validity of both the paradox of thrift and the paradox of costs. For any given real investment a_i, an increase in the propensity to save out of profits s_c will lead to a fall in output – as will a decrease in real wages w/p, for any given level of productivity T. Of course, whenever there is an increase in real investment a_i, output increases.

With respect to the multiplier, its value is now more complex, and given by $(s_c\{1-(w/p)/T\})^{-1}$. The multiplier now depends on the marginal propensity to save out of profits s_c, but also on the distribution of income, posited by the relationship between real wages and the productivity of workers.

As to employment, it is now given by:

$$N = a_i / \{s_c(T - w/p)\}$$

4.3 Further developments of the Kaleckian model

Multiple equilibria

Until now, we never really questioned the shape of the labour supply curve. In fact, we simply assumed it was a vertical line. Yet, many labour economists assume that the curve is backward-bending. At low wages, substitution effects dominate income effects, as rising wages induce individuals to join the labour force or to put in more hours of work. This portion of the curve has a positive slope, as would be the case in less industrialized economies. On the other hand, when wages are relatively high, income effects dominate, and this other portion of the curve has a negative slope.

With a positively-sloped or backward-bending labour supply curve, the short period Kaleckian model suggests the existence of two possible full employment equilibrium positions (Seccareccia, 1991). For instance, in Figure 4.2, at the wage $(w/p)_L$, the labour market is in equilibrium at point L. The amounts of labour being demanded and supplied are equal at N_{feL}; in other words there is a full employment equilibrium, but this full employment occurs at very low levels of real wages and output. By contrast, there is a

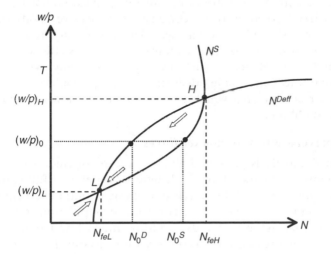

Figure 4.2: Multiple equilibria in a Kaleckian model with a backward-bending labour supply curve

second full employment equilibrium H, which corresponds to a higher real wage $(w/p)_H$, with a higher output and employment N_{feH}.

Given these two possibilities, which of the two equilibrium positions, L or H, has the highest probability of being realized? To answer this, let us consider an initial arbitrary real wage, $(w/p)_0$, which is half-way between the two full employment real wage rates. At this initial real wage, the amount of labour supplied is N_0^S, whereas the amount of labour demanded is N_0^D, that is as long as we still assume that within the short period the economy is always on the locus of points where investment equals saving (on the effective labour demand curve).

At $(w/p)_0$, the goods market is thus in equilibrium, but there is unemployment, since the labour supplied is greater than the labour demanded. For post-Keynesians, this situation could very well persist, because entrepreneurs' expectations about sales are realized and they have therefore no incentives to alter their labour hiring decisions (indeed this is the first definition of the short period). As for the real wage, provided there are sufficient institutional rigidities, it has no tendency to change as long as unemployment remains relatively stable.

This said, if the labour market were deprived of conventions, rules, regulations or institutional anchors, the nominal wage, w, would trend downwards. By contrast, the prices of goods would tend to remain stable since aggregate demand and supply are equalized, provided of course the economy is still on its effective labour demand curve. Hence, in such a flex-price economy, with falling nominal wages and stable prices, the real wage would tend to fall, until it reaches $(w/p)_L$, which corresponds to the low full employment equilibrium.

The perverse effects of market forces

Given the analysis presented above, we can conclude that if left to themselves, market forces will tend to generate a full employment equilibrium with low levels of real wages, output and employment – point L in Figure 4.2. For a given population level, this suggests that living standards would be much lower than would otherwise be the case if the economy were at point H, where high levels of real wages $(w/p)_H$, output and employment N_{feH} can be enjoyed by all.

Our analysis shows that the 'high' equilibrium is unstable, whereas the 'low' equilibrium is stable. In a world devoid of rigidities, market forces will push the economy away from the high equilibrium towards the low equilibrium, as indicated by the arrows in Figure 4.2. In other words, market forces will push the economy towards the sub-optimal equilibrium.

So, in contrast to what TINA advocates pretend, market forces and price flexibility need not generate the best of possible solutions. In this context, in times of unemployment, by preventing real wages from falling, powerful unions have beneficial effects on overall employment, production and living standards.

Since the high full-employment equilibrium is unstable, only sustained state intervention can succeed in maintaining the economy near that level of employment. In fact, the state must intervene in order to keep real wages high, even in times of rising unemployment. This could be done through minimum wage laws or living wage ordinances (as in American cities, see Pollin, 2003), with higher minimum wages pushing the entire wage structure upwards. The state can also increase wages in the public service and pass laws that encourage stronger unions that provide a countervailing force to the power of megacorporations (as in Galbraith, 1967).

While the Kaleckian multiple-equilibrium model shows that market forces can push the economy towards a low equilibrium with low levels of wages, output and employment, it also shows that adequate legislation and institutions can push the economy towards higher levels of employment, higher real wages, and higher living standards.

Technological unemployment

After having discussed a number of issues, we must address one of the oldest and most controversial issues in economics: the role played by technical progress and its impact on the level of employment. In fact, while writing his *Principles* in 1817, David Ricardo was particularly tormented by this question. While he had initially argued that technical progress would not have any permanent negative effects, he later changed his mind, as evidenced in the third edition of his book, specifically in its chapter 31.

Neoclassical authors are unanimous in arguing that technical progress can only have positive effects on employment, or at least that negative effects are only sector-specific. In fact, they ridicule those economists who warn about the potential dangers of robotics and computers on employment levels. These economists warn that technical progress can have negative effects on employment, not only on specific sectors, but at the macroeconomic level as well. Since this fear is also shared by a large number of workers, it is important that we devote some space to this issue and consider the implications of technical progress. So, the question is whether technical progress can lead to higher unemployment. Can *technological unemployment* be a macroeconomic issue?

In fact, the Kaleckian model is particularly well-suited to answering these questions. In part due to its simplicity, both in terms of graphs and equations, but also because it pays careful attention to all effects on aggregate demand.

The impact of productivity increases on the effective labour demand curve

How does an increase in productivity translate itself in a Kaleckian model? For a given real wage, any increase in labour productivity changes the distribution of income in favour of profit recipients. Without an increase in real wages, any increase in productivity translates into an increase in the costing margins of firms, θ or Θ as we called them in Chapter 2. As a result, aggregate demand falls, and hence the demand for labour also decreases. As such, the effective demand for labour curve shifts to the left, as shown by the dotted curve in Figure 4.3, where a single level of full employment has been assumed once again.

Let us start by supposing that the economy is at full employment, N_{fe}, with a given real autonomous expenditure a, productivity T_1 and real wage $(w/p)_{fe1}$. Let us now assume that productivity increases, to T_2. This will in fact shift the effective labour demand curve upwards. If this happens, full employment can be maintained, but only if real wages increase to $(w/p)_{fe2}$. However, if real wages do not change, employment necessarily falls to N_2.

Thus whenever there is an increase in productivity, there has to be some increase in real wages to keep employment from falling –

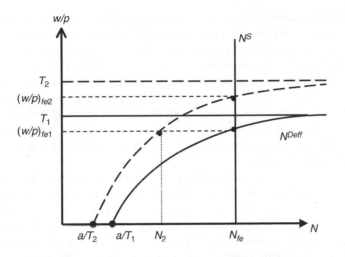

Figure 4.3:   The effect of an increase in productivity on the effective labour demand curve

that is as long as the level of real autonomous expenditures is constant, as we assumed in this model. To maintain current employment levels, the difference between productivity per worker and real wages has to be kept constant. Otherwise, real autonomous expenditures need to rise. Indeed, even when the real wage to productivity per worker ratio remains constant, meaning that real wages and productivity increase at the same rate, which would be the most probable scenario, we would still need an increase in real autonomous expenditures to keep employment at a constant level.

In the context of a Kaleckian model, therefore, technological unemployment is a real possibility. To avoid such an occurrence, the increase in productivity must usually be compensated by an increase in *both* real wages and real autonomous expenditures.

Business cycles and productivity

Which of the two following situations is most likely: real wages rising along with productivity or real wages remaining insensitive to changes in productivity? The answer to this question may depend on the stage of the business cycle.

Let us first discuss the conditions under which increases in productivity are more likely to have favourable effects on employment. If increases in productivity arise when the economy is in an expansion, and when unemployment is low, it is probable that they will not induce negative effects on labour employment, since workers will be in a favourable situation and will most likely succeed in negotiating higher real wages. Moreover, the increased economic activity is bound to encourage firms to increase their investment expenditures, whereas households might well begin to increase discretionary spending.

When increases in productivity, however, are the result of the cost-cutting efforts of firms, either because the economy is in recession or because firms or their shareholders do not think they are making enough profit, it is more than likely that these increases in productivity will have negative effects on employment. Since in this case the managers' primary objective is to increase their profit margins, it is highly unlikely that they would be willing to share productivity increases with workers. As a result, wages will not tend to increase, and firms will hesitate to invest.

These are in fact perfect examples of vicious and virtuous circles. When the economy is growing, increases in productivity resulting from economies of scale and the growing scarcity of available workers will not have any negative effects on employment. When the economy is in a recession or is stagnating, however, each firm, quite justifiably, will try to reduce its unit costs, although this will have pernicious effects on macroeconomic employment. This vicious circle of technological unemployment is similar to what occurred in continental Europe, during the 1980s and 1990s. According to post-Keynesian observers, the rising or high rates of unemployment that have been experienced in these countries cannot be attributed to the rigidity of labour markets; rather, the culprit might well be the lack of effective demand generated by restrictive macroeconomic policies designed to maintain economies within the European monetary system and then to fulfil the Maastricht criteria for entry into the eurozone (Irvin, 2005).

Box 4.7: Technological unemployment, price setting, and autonomous real demand

It is quite easy to show that even a proportional increase in real wages relative to productivity will not be sufficient to maintain existing levels of employment (Nell, 1988, p. 124). Assume that firms set prices according to the simple following mark-up condition:

$$p = (1 + \theta)(DUC)$$

In our simple Kaleckian vertically-integrated model, direct unit costs (*DUC*) are simply wage costs per unit of output. At the aggregate level, therefore, the mark-up price equation becomes:

$$p = (1 + \theta)wn = (1 + \theta)(w/T)$$

By rearranging, we get the following real wage equation:

$$w/p = T/(1 + \theta)$$

As we can see, the real wages of workers, and therefore their purchasing power, are directly related to productivity, T. They also depend inversely on the costing margin, θ. If firms do not seek to increase their costing margin when they reduce their unit costs, θ remains constant and the real wage w/p moves in proportion to productivity T. So for instance, if productivity increases, say, by 5 per cent, so do real wages.

Inserting the real-wage equation above into the effective labour demand equation defined earlier – that is into $N^{Deff} = a/\{T-(w/p)\}$ – we obtain the following:

$$N^{Deff} = a(1+ \theta) /T\,\theta$$

Even if we assume proportional increases in real wages and productivity, the effective labour demand will decrease whenever T increases. To keep the effective demand for labour constant,

---

Box 4.7: Technological unemployment, price setting, and
autonomous real demand – *cont'd*

we need in addition a proportional increase in real autonomous
expenditures, *a*. Hence, if the ratio *a/T* remains constant, for a
given costing margin θ, the effective demand for labour is
constant and the economy will then avoid technological
unemployment. These are nonetheless stringent conditions.
Thus technological unemployment cannot simply be rejected
out of hand, by invoking Say's Law or one's faith in the ability
of free markets to align real wages to the marginal productivity
of labour, as neoclassical economists do.

Work sharing

The high levels of unemployment over the last 20 years in France
and other European countries have encouraged left-of-centre and
social economists to propose some innovative policies aimed at
reducing unemployment. One such policy is work-sharing, whereby
workers reduce their hours of work with the objective of increasing
overall employment – a policy incidentally considered by Keynes
(1936, ch. 22.V) with little enthusiasm.

Work-sharing rests on the hypothesis that firms require a certain
number of work-hours in order to meet their production goals. It
presumes that if workers reduce the length of their working day or
working week, firms will have no choice but to hire additional
workers.

Yet, work-sharing has important consequences for the hourly
productivity of workers, besides its impact on employment and on
weekly or monthly wage income. Many firms claim that the adoption of a four-day working week, as an alternative to a five-day
week, has led to an increase in hourly productivity. In the best of
circumstances, workers are able to achieve in four days what they
would otherwise do in five.

If this is indeed so, and assuming further that workers have accepted a 20 per cent reduction in their weekly or monthly pay, since they have reduced their work week by one day, it implies that unit labour costs are being reduced by 20 per cent while hourly productivity is rising by a similar percentage.

The reduction of the number of working hours per week, as part of a work-sharing programme, can probably also lead to increases in productivity rates. But as we have seen in previous sections of this chapter, any increase in productivity is bound to have negative effects on employment unless it is compensated by an increase in real wages. In the extreme case of the four-day week considered above, where workers do in four days what they used to do in five days, there would be no effect whatsoever on the number of employed workers, *if effective demand could remain the same*. But effective demand *will* fall, since hourly productivity rises while the hourly real wage does not.

Work-sharing, or the four-day working week, can only have favourable effects on employment if hourly wages w/p are increased, at least in proportion with productivity gains. Otherwise, if such policies are accompanied by a reduction in weekly or monthly wages, because workers are working a lesser number of hours at the same pay rate, then they will have no beneficial effect on the demand for labour.

To be successful, a work-sharing policy must therefore be accompanied by an increase in hourly real wages, so that the annual purchasing power of each worker is maintained, thus also sustaining aggregate demand. Otherwise, the increase in hourly productivity which is likely to arise from such programmes will lead to a decrease in effective labour demand.

The best way to achieve this increase in the hourly wage is to preserve the existing weekly (or monthly) wage, despite the reduction in the official number of hours on the job. Post-Keynesians only endorse work-sharing programmes and their reduced working week when they are accompanied by an increase in the hourly real wage, that is, when the weekly wage is kept constant despite the reduction in the working week

106 *Introduction to Post-Keynesian Economics*

Box 4.8: Work-sharing, hourly labour productivity and effective demand

In our previous labour demand equations, since all variables were expressed as flows per year (for example, output per year), T stood for the output per worker per year, that is annual labour productivity, while w/p stood for the annual real wage income of a worker.

Since we now consider changes in the number of hours of work per week or per year, we must now redefine these two variables to take into account changes in the length of the working week. Let us then define:

$$T = T_h h$$

and

$$w/p = \omega_h h$$

where h is the average annual number of hours worked per worker, T_h is hourly labour productivity and ω_h is the hourly real wage.

The effective labour demand equation:

$$N^{Deff} = a/[T - (w/p)]$$

can now be rewritten as:

$$N^{Deff} = a/[T_h - \omega_h]h$$

Let us consider two extreme cases. If there is a reduction in the working week, that is a reduction in the annual number of hours worked per worker, h, with no change in both hourly productivity T_h and the hourly real wage ω_h, this will obviously lead to an increase in the overall level of employment N, and such a work-sharing programme will succeed in achieving its intended results.

Box 4.8: Work-sharing, hourly labour productivity and effective demand – *cont'd*

Suppose however, as was the case of our four-day week example, that the reduction in the length of the working week is entirely compensated by an increase in hourly productivity, so that there is no change in annual productivity T. Also, suppose, as we did with that example, that the hourly real wage ω_h is kept constant. This implies that the annual wage income of each worker $(w/p) = \omega_h h$, is now lower than before (h, the average number of annual hours of work, used to be, say, 2000 hours, at 40 hours per week for 50 weeks, whereas with the new four-day week it is 1600 hours, at 32 hours per week for 50 weeks). Looking at the $N^{Deff} = a/[T - (w/p)]$ equation, it is then obvious that employment will fall. If the annual wage income of each worker had been kept at its initial level, employment would have neither increased nor decreased.

When entrepreneurs keep costing margins θ constant despite productivity increases, that is, when hourly real wage increases are proportional to the hourly productivity gains, the effective labour demand equation becomes:

$$N^{Deff} = a(1 + \theta) /(\theta T_h h)$$

so that employment increases whenever annual productivity decreases, that is, whenever workers cannot accomplish in the shortened working week all the work that they used to do with longer hours.

5
The Long Period: Old and New Growth Models

5.1 The old post-Keynesian growth models

The Cambridge model

As stated in Chapter 1, post-Keynesians are usually known for their models of growth and distribution, developed in 1956 by such Cambridge economists as Robinson and Kaldor. The main purpose of these early models was to explain the distribution of income, more specifically the profit rate, for a given growth rate, without falling back on the standard neoclassical theory of marginal productivity.

To explain the profit rate, these old post-Keynesian models begin from a dynamic version of Kalecki's profit equation, $P = I/s_c$, developed in the previous chapter. By dividing each side by the stock of capital, K, we get the profit rate, $r = P/K$ and the growth rate $g = I/K$. Hence, from the profit equation, we get the following relationship:

$$r = g/s_c$$

which is the so-called Cambridge equation, according to which the macroeconomic profit rate is proportional to the growth rate of the economy, but inversely proportional to the propensity to save out of profits (we still assume that workers do not save).

We can of course interpret this equation as a saving function, which is exactly what we will do here. Total saving is the product of profits by the propensity to save out of profits. From this saving perspective, therefore, the growth rate of the capital stock is given by the product of two terms – the propensity to save out of profits and the profit rate. We can therefore rewrite the Cambridge equation as follows:

$$g^s = s_c r.$$

The banana diagram

Knowing what determines the profit rate, what then determines the growth rate of the economy? According to Robinson (1962), the rate of accumulation of the economy, that is the growth rate of the capital stock decided by entrepreneurs, depends on the entrepreneurs' expected or estimated profit rate, which we call r^a. Written as a linear function, her dynamic investment function can be written as follows:

$$g^i = \Delta K/K = I/K = \alpha + \beta r^a$$

Robinson herself, however, assumes that the relationship between the rate of accumulation and the expected profit rate is a non-linear one: any given increase in the rate of accumulation requires ever larger increases in the expected profit rate (the β coefficient becomes weaker).

By combining the entrepreneurs' investment function with the saving function, we get the two bold curves of Figure 5.1. This is the banana diagram, since the two curves depict an object that has the shape of a banana. Given the non-linearity of the investment function, however, the diagram yields two possible equilibrium positions; that is, there are two sets of values for which the expected profit rate is equal the realized profit rate. These two equilibria are both long-period positions.

L, which stands for the low equilibrium, is associated with low rates of profit and accumulation, and is in fact unstable. In contrast, the high equilibrium, H, is stable and reflects both a high profit rate and a high rate of accumulation. From anywhere to the right of L, the economy will eventually end up at H.

The crucial question, of course, is what makes H a stable equilibrium? To answer this question, let us assume that entrepreneurs anticipate a profit rate r^a, which is about half-way between the two possible equilibrium positions. Based on this expected profit rate, on the basis of their investment function, g^i, entrepreneurs will increase

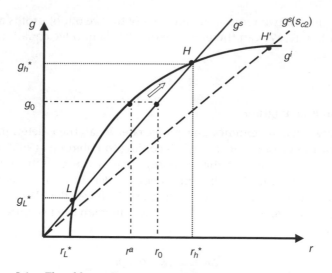

Figure 5.1:   The old post-Keynesian growth model and the paradox of thrift

their stock of capital at a rate g_0; this will generate, given the Cambridge equation above, a realized profit rate of r_0. But notice that r_0 is greater than r^a, resulting in more optimistic expected profit rates in the next period (with adaptative expectations, as long as the past is some indicator about the future). Gradually, the expected profit rate will increase until it is equal to the realized profit rate, at $r_h{}^*$, at H. The rate of accumulation will then be $g_h{}^*$.

The paradox of thrift revisited

One of the objectives of the early post-Keynesian growth models was to extend to the long period some of Keynes's insights from short-period analysis. In other words, the earlier post-Keynesians wished to provide a dynamic analogue of Keynes's static analysis. Perhaps the most important of Keynes's results was the paradox of thrift, which we outlined in the previous chapter. Let us consider it here in its dynamic form.

Before we do so, it is important to remember that in the neo-classical growth models, *à la* Solow, a fall in the propensity to save has no effect on the growth rate of the economy, although it does lead to a decrease in output per capita. In contrast, however, in the new neoclassical growth models (the so-called endogenous growth models), a decrease in the propensity to save leads to a decrease in the growth rate of the economy. This is consistent with the ideology shared by those who defend TINA: long-term gains require short-term pain.

But what do post-Keynesian growth models have to say about decreases in the propensity to save? Will they also lead to negative effects on output and growth, or is there a dynamic version of the paradox of thrift?

Figure 5.1 above allows us to verify that indeed the paradox of thrift is preserved in the post-Keynesian growth model. Consider a fall in the propensity to save, to s_{c2}. As a result, the saving curve, g^s, rotates downwards, as shown by the broken line of the g^s curve. Starting from the initial long-period equilibrium at H, with growth rate $g_h{}^*$, there will now be a realized profit rate that will be greater than the expected profit rate $r_h{}^*$. This is because, at the new lower saving rate, aggregate demand is now greater than expected. Entrepreneurs will react to this by adjusting their expected profit rate upwards and hence increasing the rate of capital accumulation. Eventually, the economy will reach the new stable equilibrium H', which is associated with a higher profit rate and a higher rate of accumulation. The paradox of thrift still holds: a lower propensity to save leads to a higher growth rate of the economy. This conclusion of course goes against one of the more fundamental tenets of TINA, according to which higher growth is only possible if households increase their saving rate. In a post-Keynesian context, however, thriftiness only results in a slowdown of the economy and lower profit rates.

A growth barrier

The old post-Keynesian growth models, however, have one feature which is questioned by Kaleckian and Sraffian economists alike. What is at stake is the necessary positive relationship between the profit rate and the gross costing margin which can be found in Kaldor's and Robinson's growth models. In their model, the increase in the profit rate that accompanies higher growth rates, arises only because of the long-period flexibility of the gross costing margin, θ or Θ as we called them in Chapter 2.

According to the early post-Keynesians, an increase in the gross costing margin is caused by long-run competitive forces. In the

1970s, post-Keynesians such as Eichner (1987) and Wood (1975) justified the existence of these forces by claiming that the leading firms in an oligopolistic market would increase their gross costing margins whenever they perceived a higher trend growth rate, as could be deduced from the description of the finance frontier in Chapter 2.

If we accept the existence of these forces, then we must also accept that for a given productivity level, an increase in the growth rate must be associated with a fall in real wages. This constitutes a barrier to growth, since workers may resist diminishing real wages by asking for higher nominal wages, thus precipitating a wage-price spiral, which Robinson (1956, p. 48) dubbed the *inflation barrier*. It is precisely this necessary negative relationship between real wages and economic growth that is rejected by contemporary Kaleckians and Sraffians.

The apparent inconsistency between Keynes and attempts at extending the *General Theory* to the long period was first discussed by Paul Davidson (1972, ch. 5). In the short period, Keynes (and Kalecki) argued that an increase in demand brings about an increase in production, and therefore an increase in the rate of capacity utilization. But in both Kaldor's and Robinson's growth models, it is explicitly assumed that the rate of utilization will return to its normal level. Any adjustment between the supply and demand for goods in the long period, or between saving and investment, is therefore done through prices and gross costing margins.

The old post-Keynesian growth models thus cannot be considered a generalization of Keynes's *General Theory* and of Kalecki's models since the transition of these growth models towards equilibrium does not involve quantity adjustments. This oversight has led to the development of new post-Keynesian growth models, which in fact are often referred to as Kaleckian growth models.

5.2 The new Kaleckian models

The new Kaleckian growth models were developed at Cambridge by Robert Rowthorn (1982) and at MIT by Amitava Dutt (1990) and Lance Taylor (1991), although the very first such model was published by Alfredo Del Monte (1975). All these models are inspired by the work of Joseph Steindl (1952), himself a student of Kalecki.

Box 5.1: The decomposition of the profit rate

One way of explaining the differences between the old and the new post-Keynesian growth models is to refer to an equation that splits the profit rate into several components. The realized profit rate, r is the ratio of realized or actual profits to the value of the stock of capital. We can rewrite it as follows:

$$r = P/K = (P/Y)(Y/Y_{fc})(Y_{fc}/K) = \pi u/v$$

Realized profit rates are thus the product of three components. These are, in order: the profit share in income ($\pi = P/Y$); the rate of capacity utilization ($u = Y/Y_{fc}$); and the inverse of the technical coefficient v, which is the ratio of the capital stock K, and full capacity income Y_{fc}.

Assuming for simplicity that v is a constant, an increase in the profit rate, r, results from either an increase in the profit share, π, or an increase in capacity utilization, u. The advocates of the old post-Keynesian growth models assumed that the rate of capacity utilization remains constant at its normal level ($u = u_n$), as discussed in Chapter 2. An increase in the profit rate, r, therefore, is only possible if the share of profit, π, increases, which is only possible if the gross costing margin θ increases. As seen in the previous chapter, this occurs when there is a decrease in the real wage w/p for any given level of productivity, T.

In contrast to the old Keynesian growth models, the profit margin of firms is a given in the new Kaleckian growth models: it is not an endogenous variable. This implies quite naturally that for a given technology, real wages are also a constant, and not taken as an endogenous variable.

The entire model is founded on the principle of effective demand, and all adjustments are done through quantities. Let us start from a short-period situation where investment is given. Now assume there is an increase in aggregate income, arising either from a decrease in the marginal propensity to save (or an increase in autonomous consumption) or from an increase in real wages. As we saw in the previous chapter, such an increase in aggregate demand will lead to an increase in production and capacity utilization.

In these Kaleckian models, such a reduction in spare capacity will encourage firms to increase their fixed capital investments; in other words, increases in capacity utilization lead to increases in the rate of accumulation (the growth rate of capital). Any increase in effective demand will lead, in the long run, to an accelerated growth rate of the economy. This is a variation on the accelerator principle, often discussed by early Keynesians such as Hicks and Samuelson.

Yet, in contrast to the early post-Keynesian models, a higher rate of accumulation will be associated with a higher rate of utilization of productive capacity. While it is true that a firm acting individually could succeed in maintaining its rate of capacity utilization around its normal level (u_n) over the long run, if all firms act in a similar way macroeconomic forces will bring about paradoxical results, with firms overall ending up producing at utilization levels either higher or lower than normal. In general, the actual rate of capacity utilization over the long run will be different from its normal rate, despite the best efforts of firms to bring back capacity to its normal degree of utilization.

A graphical representation of the Kaleckian model

As is the case with the old post-Keynesian model of growth, the Kaleckian model can be represented quite simply with only two functions: a saving and an investment function (g^i and g^s). As long as the stability condition holds, market forces will push the economy towards the intersection of these two functions.

Let us assume that workers, either through negotiations or by legislation, obtain a higher real wage despite constant productivity. This implies that the gross costing margin, θ, as well as the profit share, π, will be reduced. What will be the impact of these changes on the rate of accumulation and the profit rate in the long run?

We already know the answer to one of these questions. Indeed, the rate of accumulation will be increased. This can be seen in the upper part of Figure 5.2. The reduction in the profit share π reduces the propensity to save of the economy as a whole ($s = s_c\pi$), thereby rotating the saving function g^s downwards, as shown by the dotted g^s curve in Figure 5.2. As a first stage, at the initial accumulation rate g_0^*, sales resulting from the new distribution of income as well as

Box 5.2: A formalized version of the Kaleckian growth model

Let us consider an abridged version of the Kaleckian model presented by Edward Amadeo (1986). There are three components to this model. The first is an investment function, which is similar to Robinson's linear function, although now it depends on capacity utilization rates, and no longer (only) on the profit rate. Hence, we can write the following:

$$g^i = \alpha + \beta(u - u_n) \qquad (5.1)$$

We can interpret α as the trend growth rate of sales expected by firms. When the actual rate of utilization is equal to the normal rate of utilization u_n, firms want to increase their productive capacity at the same rate as the expected growth rate of sales, and thus we have $g^i = \alpha$. When the actual rate of utilization, however, is less than the normal rate, that is when $u - u_n < 0$, firms believe that they have excess capacity, and they will want to rectify the situation by allowing their capital stock to grow at a lesser rate, that is at a rate which is less than the expected growth rate of sales: $g^i < \alpha$. The opposite holds true whenever the rate of utilization is above the normal rate: firms now believe that they have an insufficient amount of spare capacity, and they will attempt to achieve normal rates of capacity utilization in the future by increasing their rate of accumulation above the expected growth rate of sales, hoping that they will now return to a more normal rate. The investment function does reflect the belief that, taken individually, each firm strives to return to normal rates of capacity utilization.

The other two equations in the Kaleckian growth model are in fact quite well known by now. The second equation is the Cambridge saving equation:

$$g^s = s_c r \qquad (5.2)$$

Box 5.2: A formalized version of the Kaleckian growth
model – *cont'd*

As for the third equation, we need to refer to the decomposition
of the profit rate, as done in Box 5.1. This is an accounting profit
rate, seen from the cost side (*profit cost*, *PC*). For this reason we
label it r^{PC}.

$$r^{PC} = \pi u / v \qquad (5.3)$$

In this equation, the profit share, π, is taken as an exogenous
variable, directly proportional to the costing margin, θ or Θ
in the post-Keynesian cost-plus pricing equations. In this
simplified model, with no overhead labour and constant
productivity, real wages and the profit share π move inversely
to one another.

By combining equations (5.1) and (5.2), we obtain the effective
demand constraint, which represents the locus of all equilibria
where saving equals investment. This implies that all goods produced are sold. We therefore obtain the *effective demand* profit
rate, r^{ED}. Hence, we can write:

$$r^{ED} = (\alpha - \beta u_n + \beta u)/s_c \qquad (5.4)$$

Moreover, by combining equations (5.2) and (5.3) we get
a saving equation as a function of the rate of capacity
utilization:

$$g^s = s_c \pi \, u / v \qquad (5.5)$$

We can now draw the curves representing these equations, as is
done in Figure 5.2 below, with equations (5.1) and (5.5) – the
investment and saving equations – appearing in the upper half
of the figure, while equations (5.3) and (5.4) – the profit cost
curve *PC* and the effective demand curve *ED* – are shown in the
lower half.

Box 5.2: A formalized version of the Kaleckian growth model – *cont'd*

As in the old post-Keynesian growth models, the model is stable provided the saving function is more sensitive to changes in endogenous variables (such as the rate of utilization) than is the investment function. The following condition must therefore hold:

$$s_c \, \pi/v > \beta$$

By combining either equations (5.1) and (5.5), or (5.3) and (5.4), we get the equilibrium rate of utilization:

$$u^* = (\alpha - \beta u_n)/(\, s_c \pi/v - \beta)$$

---

from the higher demand for consumption goods will correspond to the rate of utilization u_1.

These higher sales will now lead firms to anticipate higher rates of utilization, which will induce them to raise their rate of accumulation, up until the economy gets to reach g_1^*, a higher rate of accumulation, at a higher rate of utilization u_1^*. At this point, sales will exactly offset production, and a new long-period equilibrium will have been attained. The new equilibrium illustrates the paradox of thrift: the reduction in the profit share, and therefore of the aggregate propensity to save, leads to an increase in the long-period rates of accumulation and capacity utilization.

The paradox of costs

But there exists a second effect, just as important and equally surprising, which is the dynamic version of the paradox of costs, which we discussed in the previous chapter. A higher real wage, and therefore higher costs of production, leads to a higher long-period profit rate. In other words, a *reduction* in the gross costing margin of each individual firm ultimately leads to a *higher* profit rate for the economy as a whole.

We can better understand this paradox with the help of the lower part of Figure 5.2. The increase in real wages and the reduction in

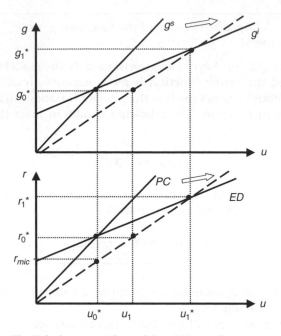

Figure 5.2: The Kaleckian growth model and its paradoxes

the profit share π can be depicted as a downward rotation in the PC curve, which represents the accounting profit rate for every rate of capacity utilization. If the rate of utilization were to remain at $u_0{}^*$, the profit rate would fall to r_{mic}, in line with the assumed lower costing margins of firms, as would be depicted by a microeconomic partial equilibrium analysis. But the actual degree of capacity does not remain at its initial level when we take into account the macroeconomic implications of the assumed change. The rate of utilization corresponding to actual sales increases to u_1, so that the short-run profit rate remains at its initial level $r_0{}^*$, despite the fall in costing margins.

In the long run, the accelerator effects spring into action. The higher rate of utilization leads to an increase in the rate of accumulation, with this latter increase feeding back into a higher profit rate. The economy eventually moves up to profit rate $r_1{}^*$, where the PC and ED curves intersect once again.

This example shows that the paradox of costs is a macroeconomic phenomenon. If a single firm raises real wages and reduces its gross costing margin, everything else being equal, it will obviously make less profit and it will face a reduction in its profit rate (unless the increase in real wages leads to an increase in productivity, as in theories of wage efficiency). But, if all firms reduce their gross costing margins, this will generate a greater rate of capacity utilization for the whole economy, and hence a higher macroeconomic profit rate.

As a result of this analysis, we may conclude the following: while it may be beneficial to an individual firm acting alone to reduce its costs of production and to increase its profit margins by reducing real wages or shedding employment (as long as this does not affect negatively the productivity of the remaining workers), the profit rate at the aggregate level could be greater if all firms agreed to reduce their gross costing margins.

The paradox of costs and the paradox of thrift are both key features of the canonical Kaleckian growth model. A reduction in the propensity to save leads to a higher rate of accumulation, while a rise in real wages gets translated into a higher profit rate at the macroeconomic level. Both results are in direct conflict with neoclassical theory and TINA. In fact, these two paradoxes are very good examples of what happens when one does not assume full employment of labour and capacity as the starting point of economic analysis. These paradoxes emphasize the importance of effective demand and that of real-world adjustments through quantities instead of prices. Most importantly, they underline the shortcomings of an analysis that would rely solely on individual behaviour within microeconomic markets, while ignoring their macroeconomic consequences. Fallacies of composition are always lurking when unintended consequences due to macroeconomic forces are not taken into account.

5.3 Extensions and criticism of the Kaleckian model

The natural growth rate and effective demand

The Kaleckian growth model presented here only takes into consideration arguments pertaining to the demand side. As such, it leaves no room for supply considerations. Yet, supply conditions should be given some weight as they also play a role. In this section, we consider some of these implications.

Let us begin with the issue of the natural growth rate, which is the sum of the rate of technical progress and the growth rate of the labour force. If the natural growth rate diverges from the actual growth rate, as defined for instance in the Kaleckian model, then the unemployment rate will either continuously increase or decrease, depending on the circumstances. If this were the case, then the Kaleckian model would appear to be under-determined: indeed, such disequilibrium states can only occur in the short run, otherwise actual rates of unemployment would either fall to zero or be incredibly high.

There are two ways to respond to this criticism. The first is to assume that labour's negotiating power, and hence the costing margin of firms, responds to the spread between the growth rate of the economy and its natural growth rate. In other words, they respond to *changes* in the unemployment rate. Under certain conditions, the endogeneity of the profit margins may in fact push the growth rate of the economy towards its natural level. Yet, effective demand is still playing an important role since stronger autonomous demand will lead to a lower unemployment rate in the long run (Stockhammer, 2004)

The second Kaleckian response to this criticism is perhaps more radical. It suggests that while supply conditions are important, it is the natural growth rate that adjusts to the actual growth rate. In other words, supply adjusts to changes in effective demand (León-Ledesma and Thirlwall, 2002). This suggests that the natural growth rate is itself an endogenous variable.

Endogenous technical progress

Assuming this suggestion is correct, then how can we justify it? There are several mechanisms that explain the endogenous nature of the natural rate. For instance, when the economy is expanding quickly, the supply of labour tends to follow suit, due to such factors as an augmentation in the number of hours worked per employee, an increase in the population's participation rate (especially among women), or increases in foreign labour immigration. But there are also other factors, which contribute to faster rates of technical progress: labour may tend to shift towards more productive sectors, economies of scale may arise, some dynamic mechanisms tied to knowledge (learning by doing) may kick in, and innovations may be adopted more quickly.

All of these factors combined suggest that the natural growth rate is an endogenous variable, adjusting to changes occurring on the demand side of the economy. The endogeneity of the natural growth rate can be interpreted as an instance of *hysteresis*, whereby actual aggregate demand growth produces a multiplicity of natural growth rates. The economy becomes path-dependent.

While one might be tempted to believe that these ideas are relatively novel, having been brought about by the new literature on non-linear dynamics, hysteresis and lock-in effects, earlier post-Keynesians also entertained the possibility of multiple natural growth rates, as the following quotes demonstrate.

> Technical progress is therefore likely to be greatest in those societies where the desired rate of expansion of productive capacity (in itself the result of innumerable decisions taken by entrepreneurs) tends to exceed most the expansion of the labour force (which, as we have seen, is itself stimulated, though only up to certain limits, by the growth in production).
>
> (Kaldor, 1960, p. 237)

> But at the same time technical progress is being speeded up to keep up with accumulation. The rate of technical progress is not a natural phenomenon that falls like the gentle rain from heaven. When there is an economic motive for raising output per man the entrepreneurs seek out inventions and improvements. Even more important than speeding up discoveries is the speeding up of the rate at which innovations are diffused. When entrepreneurs find themselves in a situation where potential markets are expanding but labour hard to find, they have every motive to increase productivity.
>
> (Robinson, 1956, p. 96)

Verdoorn's Law

The positive relationship between the growth rate of the economy and the rate of technical progress that has just been outlined, which Kaldor (1957) called the technical progress function, has been verified for a number of economies. It is known as Verdoorn's Law (McCombie and Thirlwall, 1994).

Combining Verdoorn's Law with the Kaleckian growth model yields surprising implications. Indeed, let us assume a decrease in the gross costing margin such that, everything else being equal, real wages increase. According to the Kaleckian model, this leads to an increase in effective demand and therefore an accelerated growth rate. But now, given Verdoorn's Law, this higher growth rate will lead to an increase in technical progress, that is a faster growth rate for parameter T, which represents labour productivity as defined in Chapter 4. Since real wages, for a given gross costing margin, depend on T, this suggests a higher growth rate of real wages (Lavoie, 1992a, p. 327).

Verdoorn's Law thus reinforces the paradox of costs within the Kaleckian model. A decrease in the gross costing margin and the subsequent increase in real wages will have beneficial effects, not only on the profit rate of firms, but also on the long-run rate of technical progress, the growth rate of real wages and that of the purchasing power for the population at large. Once again, we can see that the conclusions we draw from the Kaleckian model stand in stark contrast to the ideas defended by those who believe in TINA, for whom there is no gain without pain.

Variants of the investment function and social antagonisms

The Kaleckian model, as presented, carries important socio-economic and political implications. In particular, it demonstrates that the antagonism between workers and capitalists is not a prerequisite of capitalist economies. Contrary to neoclassical theory, and contrary in fact to what many Marxists and classical economists claim, there is no necessary inverse relationship between real wages and profit rates. Indeed, the Kaleckian model shows that co-operation between workers and entrepreneurs can have beneficial effects for the overall economy. Wage increases lead to increased profits. Accumulation is *wage-led*.

Many Marxist and Sraffian economists, however, question some of the conclusions of the Kaleckian model. They in fact propose slightly modified versions of the model, two of which are rather interesting and will be explored here. The first variant is based on the work of Bhaduri and Marglin (1990) and that of Kurz (1990).

These authors accept all the assumptions of the Kaleckian model, but they introduce a modified investment function. They argue that the rate of accumulation g^i not only depends on the rate of utilization, but also on the profit share, π (Bhaduri and Marglin), or on the normal profit rate, r_n, as appraised by firms (Kurz). While this change may at first appear to be fairly harmless, it has considerable implications for the paradox of costs, even though the paradox of thrift is left unscathed.

Let us then consider the impact of an increase in real wages, which then results in a smaller profit share and a lower normal profit rate. The positive impact of an increase in real wages on the consumption component of aggregate demand is now, at least partially, neutralized by the negative effects of wage increases on the investment component of aggregate demand. For some parameter values the negative effects dominate, implying that an increase in real wages leads to a decrease in the rate of accumulation, the profit rate and the rate of utilization. Accumulation is then said to be *profit-led*. With the modified investment function, the paradox of costs is no longer inevitable; it is merely a possibility.

Given these differences, the consensus among post-Keynesian and radical authors now seems to be the following (see Blecker, 2002): in practice, the negative influence of a decrease in the normal profit rate is somehow compensated by the positive impact of increased sales and producers' cash-flows. Indeed, many empirical studies seem to confirm that investment decisions are very sensitive to changes in the cash-flow of firms (Fazzari et al., 1988); and we know that higher cash-flows are closely associated with higher rates of capacity utilization.

Ultimately, it seems that saving out of wages and salaries, as well as the taxation of labour income, could eliminate the positive effects on growth of a decrease in the gross costing margin. Moreover, in an open economy, an increase in real wages (achieved through an increase in nominal wages) would reduce the competitiveness of domestic firms relative to foreign firms, and hence it would reduce the demand arising from the rest of the world. Empirical studies yield different results for different countries and different time periods, thus confirming that the paradox of costs only holds for some parameter values.

The balance of payment constraint

Given the discussion above, it is now time to relax one of the most obvious constraints imposed on the Kaleckian model so far and discuss the importance of foreign aggregate demand. In doing so, we

---

Box 5.3: The role of financial markets

For simplicity, all models presented so far have neglected the discussion of financial markets. What would happen if interest payments and financial markets were included within the post-Keynesian approach? Chapter 2 offered some glimpses into this question with the discussion of the finance frontier, according to which an increase in the real rate of interest (accompanied by an increase in the dividend rate) forces firms either to increase their profit margin or to reduce their ability to self-finance. In the standard Kaleckian model, both of these changes will carry negative consequences: the first will reduce workers' consumption, whereas the second will reduce investment.

But this is not the end of the story. Indeed, things may get more complicated if we adopt a variant of the investment functions proposed by Marglin and Bhaduri or by Kurz. With high returns on financial assets (and therefore large capital gains on financial markets), rentiers' consumption can rise to the point where the overall effect of higher real interest rates may be positive. This has been verified by Epstein (1994) and Hein and Ochsen (2003).

Finally, some authors of the French regulation school, such as Boyer (2000) and Plihon (2002), analyse the ways in which other macroeconomic paradoxes may arise when consumption out of stock-market wealth is taken into account, and when financial investors attempt to impose benchmarks on financial returns to the productive sector, such as 15 per cent returns on equity norms, in their attempt to force managers to maximize shareholder value.

The systemic monetary framework discussed in Chapter 3 is particularly well-suited to answer these questions, since it allows us to consider the debt burden of firms and the changes in households' preferences for holding different kinds of financial assets, notably stock-market equities (Lavoie and Godley, 2001–02; Taylor, 2004, ch. 8).

---

need to begin our analysis with the balance of payments. According to some post-Keynesian authors, who find Harrod's work on the open economy multiplier in an open economy setting quite inspiring – not to mention contributions by Kaldor in the 1970s – many countries could grow at a much faster rate if only they were not constrained by their balance of payments.

Indeed, according to authors like McCombie and Thirlwall (1994), most governments impose severe constraints on growth as a response to external disequilibria arising from the overly rapid growth of imports. These countries have the means and the resources to grow rapidly, and they generate a domestic aggregate demand that is actually more than sufficient to justify a strong capital accumulation. Yet, these countries are constrained by a negative current account.

It is true that a surplus in the capital account, arising from the influx of foreign capital, can easily compensate for the negative current account. But such a situation can only be a temporary one for countries other than the USA, since its currency serves as an international reserve asset. Indeed, countries cannot tolerate such current account deficits for too long because of the interest and dividends that must be paid on the accumulated external debt and foreign investments. In the long run, therefore, the current account must be balanced and imports must, at most, be equal to exports.

If we suppose that domestic exports depend on the growth rate of foreign income, and that imports depend simply on domestic income and the domestic propensity to import, then, according to post-Keynesians, the maximum growth rate of an open economy in the long run (except the USA), is given by the following equation, known as Thirlwall's Law:

$$g^{BP} = \varepsilon z/\eta$$

where g^{BP} is the maximum growth rate of an economy facing a balance of payments constraint.

This maximum growth rate is proportional to the growth rate of foreign income, z, and to ε, which is the elasticity of foreign demand for domestic goods; g^{BP} is also inversely proportional to the elasticity of demand for imports, η (elasticity is defined here as the ratio of the percentage increase in demand for a given percentage increase in income).

Many empirical studies have in fact validated this simple formula for both advanced and developing economies. In fact, among advanced economies, during the period 1960–90, the rule has

applied to all countries except the USA and Japan. The USA has
had growth rates far above those predicted by g^{BP}, partly due to the
very large current account deficit that their trading partners agree to
finance by buying US government securities. As for Japan, it has had
growth rates inferior to g^{BP}, as a result of accumulated current account
surpluses. One would suspect that the same situation has arisen in
China since 2000, with its large accumulation of foreign reserves.

The USA notwithstanding, this balance of payment constraint
carries important implications because it forces countries with high
growth rates to curtail domestic demand, just as recommended by
bureaucrats at the IMF and the World Bank. As a result, there is a
strong downward pressure on global aggregate demand.

In response to such pressures, Davidson (1982) has proposed the
adoption of international mechanisms that would force 'creditor
nations' to adjust their behaviour. In other words, the IMF or some
other international monetary institution, should force countries
with a current account surplus to increase their aggregate demand,
which would then prevent countries with strong economic growth
and current account deficits from imposing restrictive monetary and
fiscal policies.

What about inflation?

In addition to the external constraint just discussed, there exists
another constraint that merits our attention, and that could in
fact undermine the conclusions drawn from the Kaleckian growth
model: this constraint is inflation. Marxist economists Gérard
Duménil and Dominique Lévy (1999) have proposed another
variant of the Kaleckian model, which undermines its canonical
long-run results – specifically the paradox of thrift and the paradox
of costs.

According to Duménil and Lévy, when the degree of capacity
utilization exceeds its normal level, there are inflationary pressures
in the economy. This is a typical instance of demand-driven inflation. When demand is strong relative to supply at normal rates of
utilization, then there is inflation. In fact, in Duménil and Lévy's
model, the level of inflation is proportional to the discrepancy
between the actual rate of utilization and its normal level.

According to these authors, central banks adopt increasingly
austere policies as long as inflation persists. Thus, for instance,

central banks will push up (real) rates of interest as long as inflation is not brought back to zero, that is as long as the actual rate of capacity utilization exceeds its normal rate. The economy will thus face increasingly high real rates of interest. These high interest rates will eventually take their toll on the expected trend growth rate of sales (the α parameter in the investment function). High real interest rates could also slow down accumulation because firms would be denied access to bank credit, on account of their deemed overly heavy financial burden.

Keynesian in the short run, classical in the long run?

If this version is adopted, then monetary policy becomes the discretionary mechanism by which paradoxical macroeconomic forces will be countered. Incidentally, this mechanism has some similarities with the new consensus models portrayed by central banks. Monetary policies aimed at targeting inflation, for instance, will force back capacity utilization rates to their normal levels. The implications for the Kaleckian model are significant.

Indeed, as Duménil and Lévy claim, adopting such an approach to monetary policy allows them to be Kaleckian (or Keynesian) when analysing short-period fluctuations, while remaining purely classical with respect to long-run growth analysis. With their modified Kaleckian model, a decrease in the propensity to save (or an increase in real wages), despite its positive short-run effects, ultimately leads to a fall in the long-period value of the rate of accumulation and an increase in real interest rates. Duménil and Lévy manage to resurrect the views of the old classical authors, according to whom accumulation requires abstinence and frugality and a supply of loanable funds. The teachings of the 'dismal science' are back.

Post-Keynesians, however, disagree with this classical variant of the Kaleckian growth model. They believe that higher rates of utilization do not necessarily lead to rising unit costs. This view of the inflationary process is consistent with the analysis presented in Chapter 2, where the marginal and average variable cost curves of firms were described as being horizontal as long as rates of utilization remain well below full capacity. Moreover, if, in line with Verdoorn's Law, rapid growth generates productivity gains that compensate at least in part for the higher wages induced by falling

Box 5.4: A horizontal Phillips curve

The Phillips curve is probably one of the best-known relationships in economics. Traditionally, it links the rate of unemployment to the rate of price inflation or to the rate of wage inflation. More recently, its meaning has been extended to imply a positive relationship between the rate of capacity utilization and the rate of inflation. In Duménil and Lévy's (1999) model, such a positive relationship is assumed to hold in the long run. Neoclassical authors usually assume that the positive relationship only holds up in the short run, assuming the existence of a vertical long-run Phillips curve at the normal rate of utilization (which more or less corresponds to the natural rate of unemployment or to the non-accelerating inflation rate of unemployment – the NAIRU).

Most post-Keynesians reject the concept of a NAIRU, believing that, if it exists, it is not uniquely supply-determined and impervious to aggregate demand; indeed post-Keynesians even show some uneasiness with the usual short-run Phillips curve, as the following quote illustrates:

> Indeed *if* it is true that there is a unique NAIRU, that really is the end of discussion of macroeconomic policy. At present I happen *not* to believe it and there is no evidence of it. And I am prepared to express the value judgment that moderately higher inflation rates are an acceptable price to pay for lower unemployment. *But I do not accept that it is a foregone conclusion that inflation will be higher if unemployment is lower.*
>
> (Godley, 1983, p. 170)

A continuously increasing number of empirical studies now show that the short-run Phillips curve is non-linear, with a flat segment for mid-range growth rates, unemployment rates or rates of capacity utilization, as illustrated in Figure 5.3 (Eisner, 1996; Filardo, 1998). This flat range where inflation tends to remain constant, in addition to the hysteresis literature and the idea that the NAIRU is attracted towards the actual level of unemployment, as determined by aggregate demand – a conclusion also supported by a meta-analysis of empirical work (Stanley, 2004) – implies that there is a lot of room for demand

---

Box 5.4: A horizontal Phillips curve – *cont'd*

management and full employment policies. Whereas most present day central banks, notably the European Central Bank, target the economy to run around utilization rate u_m, believing that this is the only non-inflationary utilization rate, central banks should venture to test the waters, as did the Federal Reserve for a while, and push the economy closer to the u_{fc} rate shown in Figure 5.3.

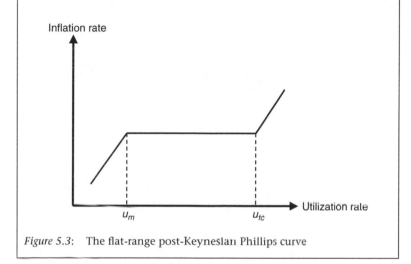

Figure 5.3: The flat-range post-Keynesian Phillips curve

---

unemployment rates, inflationary pressures will be subdued. This is precisely what happened in the USA in the late 1990s, when strong growth rates and precipitous reductions in employment rates were not accompanied by any inflationary pressures.

According to post-Keynesians, inflation is primarily a result of conflicts between social classes over the proper distribution of income, that is between rentiers, workers and entrepreneurs (Taylor, 1991, ch. 4; Cassetti, 2003). High rates of utilization lead to high profit rates, which encourage workers and their unions to make greater wage demands (Kaldor, 1985, p. 39). This is particularly the case when these high profit rates are accompanied by high growth rates and low unemployment rates. But with adequate wage bargaining institutions, there does not need to be any positive relationship between high output growth and high inflation rates (Hein, 2002). Moreover, the higher cost of raw materials induced by a world-wide boom can be dampened with the help of supranational buffer stocks. Inflation is far from being inevitable; it is the unfortunate result of inefficient institutions.

6
General Conclusion

Inspired by Keynes, post-Keynesians see capitalism as a system that encourages initiative and innovation. It can be an efficient economic system, provided it is buttressed by the state and democratic institutions capable of addressing its shortcomings and its excesses, in particular when it comes to income distribution and the provision of public services and public infrastructures to all strata of society.

One of the underlying themes running throughout this book is that, if left to itself, capitalism leads to destructive competition and waste. Without state intervention, capitalism generates instability and business cycles, and on its own can guarantee neither the full employment of labour nor a sufficient level of aggregate demand.

In contrast to neoclassical economists, post-Keynesians see this instability neither as a result of a lack of competitive forces or mechanisms, nor as a consequence of price inflexibility. On the contrary, post-Keynesians believe that price administration, conventions and legislation (such as restrictions of the free circulation of capital) actually enhance the stability of the economic system.

Post-Keynesians believe that austerity policies, the objective of which is to restrain aggregate demand in the short run (to reduce inflation, foreign deficits or the public debt, for instance) carry negative long-run effects since they decrease the productive capacity of the economy. Given the arguments presented in this book, it is necessary to reconsider the relevance of these destructive policies. It is time to reverse the priorities of most governments and central banks, by making full employment – instead of inflation – the main priority.

To maintain full employment, while still containing inflationary pressures, some post-Keynesians favour permanent incomes policies – which would include capital income (Davidson 1972, ch. 14). Other post-Keynesians favour an employment buffer-stock approach – called a 'job guarantee programme', 'employer of last resort', or 'public service employment' – whereby central government, sometimes through the intermediary of local authorities, would offer public jobs at a set wage rate to anyone willing to work and unable to find employment in the private sector (Forstater, 1998; Juniper and Mitchell, 2005). This would alleviate to some extent the terrible waste and mischief associated with involuntary labour unemployment. The advantage of this scheme, compared to the usual aggregate demand policies, is that the job guarantee programme focuses government spending where it is most needed, that is, in the regions and among the social classes where unemployment is high, thus allowing the economy to reach lower unemployment rates at steady rates of inflation.

Bibliography

Amadeo, E. (1986) 'The role of capacity utilization in long-period analysis', *Political Economy: Studies in the Surplus Approach*, 2(2), 83–94.

Andrews, P.W.S. (1949) 'A reconsideration of the theory of the individual business', *Oxford Economic Papers*, 1(1) (January), 54–89.

Arena, R. (1992) 'Une synthèse entre post-keynésiens et néo-ricardiens est-elle encore possible?', *L'actualité économique*, 68(4), 587–606.

Arestis, P. (1992) *The Post-Keynesian Approach to Economics* (Aldershot: Edward Elgar).

Arestis, P. (1996) 'Post-Keynesian economics: towards coherence', *Cambridge Journal of Economics*, 20(1), 111–35.

Arestis, P. and M. Sawyer (eds) (1994) *The Elgar Companion to Radical Political Economy* (Aldershot, UK and Brookfield, USA: Edward Elgar).

Arestis, P. and M. Sawyer (eds) (2002) *A Biographical Dictionary of Dissenting Economists*, 2nd edition (Cheltenham, UK and Northampton, MA, USA: Edward Elgar).

Arestis, P. and M. Sawyer (eds) (2006) *A Handbook of Alternative Monetary Economics* (Cheltenham, UK and Northampton, MA, USA: Edward Elgar).

Asimakopulos, A. (1975) 'A Kaleckian theory of income distribution', *Canadian Journal of Economics*, 8(3), 313–33.

Bellofiore, R. (2005) 'Monetary economics after Wicksell: alternative perspectives within the theory of the monetary circuit', in G. Fontana and R. Realfonzo (eds), *The Monetary Theory of Production: Tradition and Perspectives* (Basingstoke: Palgrave Macmillan), pp. 39–51.

Bellofiore, R. and P. Ferri (eds) (2001) *The Economic Legacy of Hyman Minsky*, 2 volumes, (Cheltenham, UK and Northampton, MA, USA: Edward Elgar).

Bhaduri, A. (1986) *Macro-economics: the Dynamics of Commodity Production* (Armonk, NY: M.E. Sharpe).

Bhaduri, A. and S. Marglin (1990) 'Unemployment and the real wage: the economic basis for contesting political ideologies', *Cambridge Journal of Economics*, 14(4), 375–93.

Blecker, R. (2002) 'Distribution, demand and growth in neo-Kaleckian macro-models', in M. Setterfield (ed.), *The Economics of Demand-led Growth: Challenging the Supply-side Vision in the Long Run* (Cheltenham, UK and Northampton, MA, USA: Edward Elgar), pp. 129–52.

Bloch, H. and M. Olive (1995) 'Can simple rules explain pricing in Australian manufacturing?', *Australian Economic Papers*, 35, 1–19.

Boggio, L. (1980) 'Full cost and Sraffa prices: equilibrium and stability in a system with fixed capital', *Economic Notes*, 9, 3–33.

Boyer, R. (1990) *The Regulation School* (New York: Columbia University Press).

Boyer, R. (2000) 'Is a finance-led growth regime a viable alternative to Fordism? A preliminary analysis', *Economy and Society*, 29(1), 111–45.

133

Brunner, E. (1975) 'Competitive prices, normal costs and industrial stability', in P.W.S. Andrews and E. Brunner, *Studies in Pricing* (London: Macmillan), pp. 18–34.

Cassetti, M. (2003) 'Bargaining power, effective demand and technical progress: a Kaleckian model of growth', *Cambridge Journal of Economics*, 27(3), 449–64.

Cecchetti, S.G. (2006) *Money, Banking, and Financial Markets* (New York: McGraw-Hill).

Chandler, A.D. (1977) *The Visible Hand: the Managerial Revolution in American Business* (Cambridge, MA: Harvard University Press).

Cohen, A. and G.C. Harcourt (2003) 'Whatever happened to the Cambridge capital theory controversies?', *Journal of Economic Perspectives*, 17(1), 199–214.

Colander, D. (2003) 'Post Walrasian macro policy and the economics of muddling through', *International Journal of Political Economy*, 33(2), 17–35.

Copeland, M.A. (1949) 'Social accounting for moneyflows', *Accounting Review*, 24 (July), 254–64. Reprinted in J.C. Dawson (ed.) (1996) *Flow-of-funds Analysis: a Handbook for Practitioners* (Armonk, NY: M.E. Sharpe).

Coutts, K., W. Godley and W. Nordhaus (1978) *Industrial Pricing in the United Kingdom* (Cambridge: Cambridge University Press).

Davidson, P. (1972) *Money and the Real World* (London: Macmillan).

Davidson, P. (1982) *International Money and the Real World* (London: Macmillan).

Davidson, P. (1984) 'Reviving Keynes's revolution', *Journal of Post Keynesian Economics*, 6(4) (Summer), 561–75.

Davidson, P. (1988) 'A technical definition of uncertainty and the long-run non-neutrality of money', *Cambridge Journal of Economics*, 12(3), 329–37.

Davidson, P. (2005) 'Responses to Lavoie, King, and Dow on what Post Keynesianism is and who is a Post Keynesian', *Journal of Post Keynesian Economics*, 27(3), 393–408.

Deleplace, G. and E.J. Nell (eds) (1996) *Money in Motion: the Post Keynesian and Circulationist Approaches* (London: Macmillan).

Del Monte, A. (1975) 'Grado di monopolio e sviluppo economico', *Rivista Internazionale di Scienze Sociali*, 46(3), 231–63.

Dostaler, G. (1988) 'La théorie post-keynésienne, la *Théorie générale* et Kalecki', *Cahiers d'économie politique*, 14–15, 123–42.

Dow, S.C. (2001) 'Post Keynesian methodology', in R.P.F. Holt and S. Pressman (eds), *A New Guide to Post Keynesian Economics* (Armonk, NY: M.E. Sharpe), pp. 11–20.

Dow, A.C and S.C. Dow (1989) 'Endogenous money creation and idle balances', in J. Pheby (ed.), *New Directions in Post-Keynesian Economics* (Aldershot, UK and Brookfield, USA: Edward Elgar), pp. 147–64.

Drakopoulos, S.A. (1992) 'Keynes's economic thought and the theory of consumer behaviour', *Scottish Journal of Political Economy*, 39(3), 318–36.

Drakopoulos, S.A. (1994) 'Hierarchical choice in economics', *Journal of Economic Surveys*, 8(2), 133–53.

Duménil, G. and D. Lévy (1993) *The Economics of the Profit Rate* (Aldershot, UK and Brookfield, USA: Edward Elgar).

Duménil, G. and D. Lévy (1999) 'Being Keynesian in the short term and classical in the long term: the traverse to classical long-term equilibrium', *The Manchester School*, 67(6), 684–716.

Dutt, A.K. (1990) *Growth, Distribution and Uneven Development* (Cambridge: Cambridge University Press).

Dutt, A.K. (2003) 'On Post Walrasian economics, macroeconomic policy and heterodox economics', *International Journal of Political Economy*, 33(2), 47–67.

Dutt, A.K. and E.J. Amadeo (1990) *Keynes's Third Alternative? The Neo-Ricardian Keynesians and the Post Keynesians* (Aldershot, UK and Brookfield, USA: Edward Elgar).

Earl, P.E. (1983) *The Economic Imagination: Towards a Behavioural Analysis of Choice* (Brighton: Wheatsheaf Books).

Eichner, A.S. (1976) *The Megacorp and Oligopoly: Microfoundations of Macro Dynamics* (Cambridge: Cambridge University Press).

Eichner, A.S. (1987) *The Macrodynamics of Advanced Market Economies* (Armonk, NY: M.E. Sharpe).

Eichner, A.S. and J.A. Kregel (1975) 'An essay on post-Keynesian theory: a new paradigm in economics', *Journal of Economic Literature*, 13(4), 1293–311.

Eisner, R. (1996). 'The retreat from full employment', in P. Arestis (ed.), *Employment, Economic Growth and the Tyranny of the Market: Essays in Honour of Paul Davidson*, vol. 2 (Cheltenham, UK and Brookfield, USA: Edward Elgar), pp. 106–30.

Epstein, G.A. (1994) 'A political economy model of comparative central banking', in G. Dymski and R. Pollin (eds), *New Perspectives in Monetary Economy* (Ann Arbor: University of Michigan Press), pp. 231–77.

Fazzari, S.M., G.R. Hubbard and B. Petersen (1988) 'Financing constraints and corporate investment', *Brookings Papers on Economic Activity*, 1, 141–95.

Filardo, A.J. (1998) 'New evidence on the output cost of fighting inflation', *Federal Reserve Bank of Kansas City Quarterly Review*, 83(3), 33–61

Fontana, G. and B. Gerrard (2004) 'A post Keynesian theory of decision-making under uncertainty', *Journal of Economic Psychology*, 25(5), 619–37.

Forstater, M. (1998) 'Flexible full employment: structural implications of discretionary public sector employment', *Journal of Economic Issues*, 32(2) 557–64.

Fullbrook, E. (ed.) (2003) *The Crisis in Economics: the Post-autistic Movement* (London: Routledge).

Galbraith, J.K. (1958) *The Affluent Society* (London: Hamish Hamilton).

Galbraith, J.K. (1967) *The New Industrial State* (New York: Houghton Mifflin).

Garegnani, P. (1990) 'Quantity of capital', in J. Eatwell, M. Milgate and P. Newman (eds), *Capital Theory* (London: Macmillan), pp. 1–78.

Georgescu-Roegen, N. (1966) *Analytical Economics* (Boston: Harvard University Press).

Godley, W. (1983) 'Keynes and the management of real national income and expenditure', in D. Worswick and J. Trevithick (eds), *Keynes and the Modern World* (Cambridge: Cambridge University Press), pp. 135–77.

Godley, W. (1999) 'Money and credit in a Keynesian model of income determination', *Cambridge Journal of Economics*, 23(4), 393–411.

Godley, W. and F. Cripps (1983) *Macroeconomics* (London: Fontana).

Godley, W. and M. Lavoie (2005–06) 'Comprehensive accounting in simple open economy macroeconomics with endogenous sterilization or flexible exchange rates', *Journal of Post Keynesian Economics*, 28(2), 241–76.

Gordon, M.J. (1997) 'A Keynesian theory of finance and its macroeconomic implications', in G.C. Harcourt and P. Riach (eds), *A Second Edition of the General Theory*, vol. 2 (London: Routledge), pp. 79–101.

Graziani, A. (2003) *The Monetary Theory of Production* (Cambridge: Cambridge University Press).

Halevi, J. and P. Kriesler (1991) 'Kalecki, classical economics and the surplus approach', *Review of Political Economy*, 3(1), 79–92.

Hall, R.L. and C.J. Hitch (1939) 'Price theory and business behaviour', *Oxford Economic Papers*, 1(2), 12–45.

Hamouda, O. and G.C. Harcourt (1988) 'Post Keynesianism: from criticism to coherence', *Bulletin of Economic Research*, 40(1), 1–33.

Hein, E. (2002) 'Monetary policy and wage bargaining in the EMU: restrictive ECB policies, high unemployment, nominal wage restraint and inflation above the target', *Banca del Lavoro Quarterly Review*, 222, 299–337.

Hein, E. and K. Ochsen (2003) 'Regimes of interest rates, income shares, savings and investment: a Kaleckian model and empirical estimations for some advanced economies', *Metroeconomica*, 54(4), 404–33.

Heiner, R.A. (1983) 'The origin of predictable behavior', *American Economic Review*, 73(4), 560–95.

Heinsohn, G. and O. Steiger (2000) 'The property theory of interest and money', in J. Smithin (ed.), *What is Money?* (London: Routledge), pp. 67–100.

Hicks, J. (1974) *The Crisis in Keynesian Economics* (Oxford: Basil Blackwell).

Holt, R.P.F. and S. Pressman (eds) (2001) *A New Guide to Post Keynesian Economics* (Armonk, NY: M.E. Sharpe).

Ironmonger, D.S. (1972) *New Commodities and Consumer Behaviour* (Cambridge: Cambridge University Press).

Irvin, G. (2005) 'The implosion of the Brussels economic consensus', Working paper 11, International Centre for Economic Research, University of Turin.

Juniper, J. and B. Mitchell (2005) 'Towards a spatial Keynesian macroeconomics', Working paper 05–09, Center for Full Employment and Equity, University of Newcastle.

Kaldor, N. (1956) 'Alternative theories of distribution', *Review of Economic Studies*, 23 (March), 83–100.

Kaldor, N. (1957) 'A model of economic growth', *Economic Journal*, 67 (December), 591–624.

Kaldor, N. (1960) 'Characteristics of economic development', in *Essays on Economic Stability and Growth* (London: Duckworth), pp. 233–42.

Kaldor, N. (1976) 'Inflation and recession in the world economy', *Economic Journal*, 86 (December), 703–14.

Kaldor, N. (1982) *The Scourge of Monetarism* (Oxford: Oxford University Press).

Kaldor, N. (1983) 'Keynesian economics after fifty years', in D. Worswick and J. Trevithick (eds), *Keynes and the Modern World* (Cambridge: Cambridge University Press), pp. 1–48

Kaldor, N. (1985) *Economics without Equilibrium* (Armonk, NY: M.E. Sharpe).

Kalecki, M. (1971) *Selected Essays on the Dynamics of the Capitalist Economy* (Cambridge: Cambridge University Press).

Keynes, J.M. (1930) *The Treatise on Money*, 2 vols (London: Macmillan).

Keynes, J.M. (1936) *The General Theory of Employment, Interest, and Money* (London: Macmillan).

Keen, S. (2001) *Debunking Economics: the Naked Emperor of the Social Sciences* (London: Zed Books).

King, J.E. (1995a) *Conversations with Post Keynesians* (London: Macmillan).

King, J.E. (1995b) *Post Keynesian Economics: an Annotated Bibliography* (Aldershot, UK and Brookfield, USA: Edward Elgar).

King, J.E. (2002) *A History of Post Keynesian Economics since 1936* (Cheltenham, UK and Northampton, MA, USA: Edward Elgar).

King, J.E. (ed.) (2003) *The Elgar Companion to Post Keynesian Economics* (Cheltenham, UK and Northampton, MA, USA: Edward Elgar).

Kurz, H. (1990) 'Technical change, growth and distribution: a steady-state approach to unsteady growth', in *Capital, Distribution and Effective Demand* (Cambridge: Polity Press), pp. 210–33.

Kurz, H. (1994) 'Growth and distribution', *Review of Political Economy*, 6(4), 393–421.

Lancaster, K. (1971) *Consumer Demand: a New Approach* (New York: Columbia University Press).

Lanzillotti, R.F. (1958) 'Pricing objectives in large companies', *American Economic Review*, 48(5), 921–40.

Lavoie, M. (1992a) *Foundations of Post-Keynesian Economic Analysis* (Aldershot, UK and Brookfield, USA: Edward Elgar).

Lavoie, M. (1992b) 'Towards a new research programme for post-Keynesianism and neo-Ricardianism', *Review of Political Economy*, 4(1), 37–78.

Lavoie, M. (1996–97) 'Real wages, employment structure, and the aggregate demand curve in a Kaleckian short-run model', *Journal of Post Keynesian Economics*, 19(2), 275–88.

Lavoie, M. (2001) 'The reflux mechanism and the open economy', in L.-P. Rochon and M. Vernengo (eds), *Credit, Interest Rates and the Open Economy* (Cheltenham, UK and Northampton, MA, USA: Edward Elgar), pp. 215–42.

Lavoie, M. (2003) 'A primer on endogenous credit-money', in L.-P. Rochon and S. Rossi (eds), *Modern Theories of Money: the Nature and Role of Money in*

Capitalist Economies (Cheltenham, UK and Northampton, MA, USA: Edward Elgar), pp. 506–43.

Lavoie, M. and W. Godley (2001–02) 'Kaleckian models of growth in a coherent stock-flow monetary framework: a Kaldorian view', *Journal of Post Keynesian Economics*, 24(2), 277–312.

Le Bourva, J. (1992) [1962] 'Money creation and money multipliers, *Review of Political Economy*, 4(4), 447–62.

Lee, F. (1998) *Post-Keynesian Price Theory* (Cambridge: Cambridge University Press).

Leibenstein, H. (1978) *General X-efficiency Theory and Economic Development* (Oxford: Oxford University Press).

Leijonhufvud, A. (1976) 'Schools, revolutions and research programmes in economic theory', in S.J. Latsis (ed.), *Method and Appraisal in Economics* (Cambridge: Cambridge University Press), pp. 65–108.

León-Ledesma, M.A. and A.P. Thirlwall (2002) 'The endogeneity of the natural rate of growth', *Cambridge Journal of Economics*, 26(4), 441–59.

Lucas, R. (1981) *Studies in Business Cycle Theory* (Cambridge, MA: MIT Press).

Lutz, M.A. and K. Lux (1979) *The Challenge of Humanistic Economics* (Menlo Park, CA: Benjamin/Cummings).

Marris, R. (1964) *The Economic Theory of Managerial Capitalism* (New York: Free Press of Glencoe).

McCombie, J.S.L. and A.P. Thirlwall (1994) *Economic Growth and the Balance-of-payments Constraint* (New York: St Martin's Press).

Means, G. (1936) 'Notes on inflexible prices', *American Economic Review*, 26(1), 23–35.

Minsky, H.P. (1976) *John Maynard Keynes* (London: Macmillan).

Minsky, H.P. (1981) *Can 'It' Happen Again? Essays on Instability and Finance* (Armonk, NY: M.E Sharpe).

Mongiovi, G. (1991) 'Keynes, Sraffa and the labour market', *Review of Political Economy*, 3(1), 25–42.

Moore, B.J. (1988) *Horizontalists and Verticalists: the Macroeconomics of Credit Money* (Cambridge: Cambridge University Press).

Nell, E.J. (1988) *Prosperity and Public Spending: Transformational Growth and the Role of Government*, (Boston: Hyman).

Nell, E.J. (1992) *Transformational Growth and Effective Demand* (London: Macmillan).

Nell, E.J. (1998) *The Theory of Transformational Growth: Keynes after Sraffa* (Cambridge: Cambridge University Press).

Okun, A.M. (1981) *Prices and Quantities* (Washington: Brookings Institution).

Palley, T. (1996) *Post Keynesian Economics: Debt, Distribution and the Macro Economy* (London: Macmillan).

Panico, C. (1988) *Interest and Profit in the Theories of Value and Distribution* (London: Macmillan).

Parguez, A. (2001) 'Money without scarcity: from the horizontalist revolution to the theory of the monetary circuit', in L.-P. Rochon and M. Vernengo (eds), *Credit, Interest Rates and the Open Economy: Essays on Horizontalism* (Cheltenham, UK and Northampton, MA, USA: Edward Elgar), pp. 69–103.

Pasinetti, L.L. (1977) *Lectures on the Theory of Production* (London: Macmillan).

Pasinetti, L.L. (1981) *Structural Change and Economic Growth* (Cambridge: Cambridge University Press).

Pasinetti, L.L. (1993) *Structural Economic Dynamics* (Cambridge: Cambridge University Press).

Pasinetti, L.L. (2005) 'The Cambridge School of Keynesian economics', *Cambridge Journal of Economics*, 29(6), 837–48.

Penrose, E. (1959) *The Theory of the Growth of the Firm* (Oxford: Basil Blackwell).

Pivetti, M. (1985) 'On the monetary explanation of distribution', *Political Economy: Studies in the Surplus Approach*, 1(2), 73–103.

Plihon, D. (2002) *Rentabilité et risque dans le nouveau régime de croissance* (Paris: La Documentation française)

Pollin, R. (2003) 'Evaluating living wage laws in the United States: good intentions and economic reality in conflict?', Working Paper 61, PERI, University of Massachusetts, Amherst.

Reynolds, P.J. (1987) *Political Economy: a Synthesis of Kaleckian and Post Keynesian Economics* (Brighton: Wheatsheaf).

Robinson, J. (1956) *The Accumulation of Capital* (London: Macmillan).

Robinson, J. (1962) *Essays in the Theory of Economic Growth* (London: Macmillan).

Robinson, J. (1971) *Economic Heresies* (London: Macmillan).

Robinson, J. (1973). 'The second crisis of economic theory', in J. Robinson, *Collected Economic Papers*, vol. IV (Oxford: Basil Blackwell), pp. 92–105.

Robinson, J. (1980) 'Time in economic theory', *Kyklos*, 33(2), 219–29.

Rochon, L.P. (1999) *Credit, Money and Production: an Alternative Post-Keynesian Approach* (Cheltenham, UK and Northampton, MA, USA: Edward Elgar).

Rochon, L.P. and S. Rossi (eds) (2003) *Modern Theories of Money: the Nature and Role of Money in Capitalist Economies* (Cheltenham, UK and Northampton, MA, USA: Edward Elgar).

Roncaglia, A. (1995) 'On the compatibility between Keynes's and Sraffa's viewpoints on output levels', in G. Harcourt, A. Roncaglia and R. Rowley (eds), *Income and Employment in Theory and Practice* (London: Macmillan), pp. 111–25.

Roncaglia, A. (2003) 'Energy and market power: an alternative approach to the economics of oil', *Journal of Post Keynesian Economics*, 25(4), 641–60.

Rogers, C. (1989) *Money, Interest and Capital: a Study in the Foundations of Monetary Theory* (Cambridge: Cambridge University Press).

Rosser, J.B. (1998) 'Complex dynamics in New Keynesian and Post Keynesian Economics', in R.J. Rotheim (ed.), *New Keynesian Economics/Post Keynesian Alternatives* (London: Routledge), pp. 288–302.

Rotheim, R.J. (ed.) (1996) *New Keynesian Economics/Post Keynesian Alternatives* (London: Routledge).

Rowthorn, B. (1982) 'Demand, real wages and economic growth', *Studi Economici*, 18, 3–54.

Roy, R. (2005) 'The hierarchy of needs and the concept of groups in consumer choice theory (1943)', *History of Economics Review*, 42 (Summer), 50–6.

Sawyer, M. (1989) *The Challenge of Radical Political Economy: an Introduction to the Alternatives to Neo-classical Economics* (New York: Harvester Wheatsheaf).

Sawyer, M. (1995) 'Comment on Earl and Shapiro', in S. Dow and J. Hillard (eds), *Keynes, Knowledge and Uncertainty* (Cheltenham, UK and Brookfield, USA: Edward Elgar), pp. 303–11.

Schefold, B. (1997) *Normal Prices, Technical Change and Accumulation* (London: Macmillan).

Seccareccia, M. (1991) 'Salaire minimum, emploi et productivité dans une perspective post-keynésienne', *L'Actualité économique*, 67(2), 166–91.

Setterfield, M. (2003) 'What is analytical political economy?', *International Journal of Political Economy*, 33(2), 4–16.

Shapiro, N. (1977) 'The revolutionary character of post-Keynesian economics', *Journal of Economic Issues*, 11(3), 541–60.

Simon, H.A. (1976) 'From substantive to procedural rationality', in S.J. Latsis (ed.), *Method and Appraisal in Economics* (Cambridge: Cambridge University Press), pp. 129–48.

Smithin, J. (2003) *Controversies in Monetary Economics*, 2nd edition (Cheltenham, UK and Northampton, MA, USA: Edward Elgar).

Spash, C.L. and N. Hanley (1995) 'Preferences, information and biodiversity preservation', *Ecological Economics*, 12(3), 191–208.

Sraffa, P. (1960) *The Production of Commodities by Means of Commodities* (Cambridge: Cambridge University Press).

Stanley, T.D. (2004) 'Does unemployment hysteresis falsify the natural rate hypothesis? A meta-regression analysis', *Journal of Economic Surveys*, 18(4), 589–612.

Steedman, I. (1977) *Marx after Sraffa* (London: New Left Books).

Steindl, J. (1952) *Maturity and Stagnation in American Capitalism* (Oxford: Basil Blackwell).

Stiglitz, J.E. (2002) *Globalization and its Discontents* (New York: W.W. Norton).

Stiglitz, J.E. (2003) *The Roaring Nineties* (New York: W.W. Norton).

Stockhammer, E. (2004) 'Is there an equilibrium rate of unemployment in the long run?', *Review of Political Economy*, 16(1), 59–78.

Sylos Labini, P. (1971) 'The theory of prices in oligopoly and the theory of growth', in P. Sylos Labini, *The Forces of Economic Growth and Decline* (Cambridge, MA: MIT Press), pp. 123–45.

Taylor, J.B. (2004) *Principles of Macroeconomics*, 4th edition (New York: Houghton Mifflin).

Taylor, L. (1991) *Income Distribution, Inflation, and Growth: Lectures on Structuralist Macroeconomic Theory* (Cambridge, MA: MIT Press).

Taylor, L. (2004) *Reconstructing Macroeconomics: Structuralist Proposals and Critiques of the Mainstream* (Cambridge, MA: Harvard University Press).

Tobin, J. (1979) *Asset Accumulation and Economic Activity* (New Haven, CT: Yale University Press).

Tobin, J. (1982) 'Money and finance in the macroeconomic process', *Journal of Money, Credit, and Banking*, 14(2), 171–204.

Van Ees, H. and H. Garretsen (1993) 'On the contribution of New Keynesian economics', *De Economist*, 141(3), 323–52.

Ventelou, B. (2001) *Au-delà de la rareté: la croissance économique comme construction sociale* (Paris: Albin Michel).

Vickrey, W. (1997) 'A trans-Keynesian manifesto', *Journal of Post Keynesian Economics*, 19(4), 495–510.

Walters, B. and D. Young (1999) 'On the coherence of post-Keynesian economics', *Scottish Journal of Political Economy*, 44(3), 329–49.

Wolfson, M.H. (1996) 'A post Keynesian theory of credit rationing', *Journal of Post Keynesian Economics*, 18(3), 443–70.

Wolfson, M. (2003) 'Credit rationing', in J. King (ed.), *The Elgar Companion to Post Keynesian Economics* (Cheltenham, UK and Northampton, MA, USA: Edward Elgar), pp. 77–82.

Wood, A. (1975) *A Theory of Profits* (Cambridge: Cambridge University Press).

Wray, L.R. (1990) *Money and Credit in Capitalist Economies: the Endogenous Money Approach* (Aldershot, UK and Brookfield, USA: Edward Elgar).

Index